I0538382

I AM AN
AMERICAN

A Citizen's Guide to the Documents,
Speeches, and Ideals That Shaped America

Compiled and Edited by Brendan Cherry

Copyright © 2026 Proclaiming Truth Publications.
All Scripture quotations are taken from the King James Version.
Special emphasis in verses is added.

Published in 2026 by Proclaiming Truth Publications, a ministry
of Canaan Baptist Church, Covington, GA.

All rights reserved. No part of this book may be reproduced,
stored in a retrieval system, or transmitted in any form or by
any means–electronic, mechanical, photocopy, recording, or
otherwise–without written permission of the publisher, except for
brief quotations in printed reviews.

PROCLAIMING TRUTH
publications

5581 Salem Road
Covington, GA 30016
770.786.8885

Cover design and layout by Brendan Cherry

The author and publication team have put forth every effort to give
proper credit to quotes and thoughts that are not original with the
author. It is not our intent to claim originality with any quote or
thought that could not readily be tied to an original source.

Table of Contents

Introduction

As I write these words, we celebrate the 250th year of the United States of America—a remarkable milestone in the story of freedom. Yet, in this season, our nation faces deep internal turmoil. Political divisions, cultural unrest, and moral challenges have left many questioning the direction of our country. Now, more than ever, we need a revival of patriotism, a renewed love for our country, and a commitment to the principles that have made America exceptional.

America is not perfect. It never has been. But there is no better place to live. This is the land of the free and the home of the brave. The liberties we enjoy, the opportunities available to us, and the blessings of our heritage were hard-won and preserved through the courage, sacrifice, and vision of those who came before us.

This book is designed to inspire a renewed love and appreciation for America by helping readers understand what it truly means to be an American. Within these pages, you will find core American documents, historic speeches, patriotic poems, and reminders of the legacy entrusted to us by our founders and the generations who preceded us.

Each piece is chosen to awaken both heart and mind to the responsibilities and privileges of citizenship.

For Christians, this book carries a special challenge. Far too often, believers take a backseat in civic life, assuming that engagement in politics is somehow separate from their spiritual calling. Yet Scripture teaches otherwise.

And they send unto him certain of the Pharisees and of the Herodians, to catch him in his words. And when they were come, they say unto him, Master, we know that thou art true, and carest for no man: for thou regardest not the person of men, but teachest the way of God in truth: Is it lawful to give tribute to Caesar, or not? Shall we give, or shall we not give? But he, knowing their hypocrisy, said unto them, Why tempt ye me? bring me a penny, that I may see it. And they brought it. And he saith unto them, Whose is this image and superscription? And they said unto him, Caesar's. And Jesus answering said unto them, Render to Caesar the things that are Caesar's, and to God the things that are God's. And they marvelled at him (Mark 12:13-17).

In Mark 12:13–17, Jesus confronted the Pharisees and Herodians who tried to trap Him with a false choice: God or government. Jesus' answer revealed a profound truth—obedience to God is not the opposite of submission to government. In fact, fulfilling our civic duties is part of living faithfully under God's authority.

The Apostle Paul reinforced this in Romans 13 and 1 Peter 2:13–17, reminding believers that government is ordained by God and that submission to lawful authority, along with the responsible exercise of civic duties, is a part of living righteously. In a republic like ours, *"rendering unto Caesar"* takes on an added dimension—because in

America, *"Caesar"* is us—we the people. Voting, advocacy, stewardship, and civic engagement are not political distractions—they are spiritual responsibilities.

Christianity and citizenship are not at odds. They are inseparably linked. Our faith calls us to be salt and light in the world, and that includes the public square. From our local school boards to our national elections, from the choices we make in our daily lives to the way we interact with our neighbors, the Bible calls us to actively influence the society in which we live. The consequences of apathy are real. When believers sit idly by, the foundations of our freedom erode, leaving the door open for ideologies that oppose God's design.

This book will guide you to see America not only as a nation of laws and governance but also as a divinely favored experiment in liberty, where faith, family, and freedom intersect. As Christians, we are challenged to remain vigilant, pray, and vote; to take seriously the responsibilities entrusted to every citizen; and to consider the eternal implications of how you engage with the society around you.

Our founding fathers understood these truths. They prayed, they debated, they sacrificed, and they designed a government of the people, by the people, and for the people—a government that could endure through the centuries if its citizens remained vigilant, virtuous, and engaged. It is now our turn to rise to that call.

As you read this book, may you be inspired to love your country, honor the sacrifices of those who built it, and embrace the responsibility of citizenship with courage, conviction, and faith. May your heart burn with a renewed appreciation for America, and may your life reflect the profound truth that in serving our country well, we serve God faithfully.

We are Americans. The freedoms we enjoy are gifts—both a privilege and a responsibility. Let us live worthy of them.

May God Bless America.

Part One

THE AMERICAN IDEA

What it means to be American

Americanism

I AM AN AMERICAN. I embrace this idea of Americanism.

Americanism is the heartbeat of what makes America special—a powerful blend of freedom, faith, and fierce self-reliance that no other nation on earth can claim.

Unlike any other country, America wasn't built on bloodlines, ancient traditions, or a single ethnic story. It was built on an idea: that every person is created by God with certain rights that no king, no government, no tyrant can take away—life, liberty, and the pursuit of happiness. That single revolutionary truth, declared in 1776, set this nation apart. Americanism means living out that truth every day.

It means you are free to worship God openly, to work hard, to build something great with your own hands, to speak your mind, to raise your family according to your convictions—all without some distant bureaucracy telling you how to live. It's the conviction that government exists to protect your God-given rights, not to control your life, your wallet, your church, or your conscience.

Americanism is rugged individualism wrapped in moral

courage. It's the pioneer spirit that crossed oceans and prairies trusting in Providence. It's the farmer rising before dawn, the inventor burning the midnight oil, the parent teaching their children right from wrong, the soldier standing watch—all driven by the belief that you answer first to God, then to your own conscience, and only then to lawful authority.

This way of life has produced miracles: a free people who turned a wilderness into the most prosperous, generous, and innovative nation in history. It's given ordinary men and women extraordinary opportunities to dream big, to fail and rise again, to help their neighbor without being forced, and to spread the Gospel to the ends of the earth.

To be an American is an astonishing privilege. You stand on ground soaked in the prayers and sacrifices of generations who believed liberty under God was worth everything. That legacy isn't automatic—it's a torch passed to us. We keep it burning by staying true to those founding principles: faith in God, love of freedom, personal responsibility, and gratitude for this one-of-a-kind country.

America is still that shining city on a hill. Let's live like it— boldly, gratefully, and unapologetically—so the world can see what a people set free by God can accomplish.

The American's Creed

I believe in the United States of America as a government of the people, by the people, for the people; whose just powers are derived from the consent of the governed, a democracy in a republic, a sovereign Nation of many sovereign States; a perfect union, one and inseparable; established upon those principles of freedom, equality, justice, and humanity for which American patriots sacrificed their lives and fortunes.

I therefore believe it is my duty to my country to love it, to support its Constitution, to obey its laws, to respect its flag, and to defend it against all enemies.

— William Tyler Page

In God We Trust

Few phrases capture the American spirit more clearly than these four words: *In God We Trust*. They are familiar, often overlooked, and sometimes dismissed as ceremonial. But from the beginning of our nation, this phrase has represented far more than tradition. It reflects a deeply held conviction—that the success, survival, and future of America depend upon a firm reliance on God.

Scripture reminds us, *"Blessed is the nation whose God is the Lord"* (Psalm 33:12). That truth was not merely believed by early Americans—it was lived, proclaimed, and embedded into the very institutions of the nation.

THE ORIGIN OF THE PHRASE

The phrase *In God We Trust* first appeared during one of the darkest periods in American history—the Civil War. In 1861, as the nation was torn apart by bloodshed and uncertainty, Americans were acutely aware of their need for divine help.

A letter sent to the United States Treasury urged that God be acknowledged on the nation's coinage, declaring that such recognition would *"relieve us from the ignominy of heathenism"* and serve as a public testimony that the United States was a nation under God.

Treasury Secretary Salmon P. Chase agreed. In a written directive to the Director of the Mint, Chase stated:

> *"No nation can be strong except in the strength of God, or safe except in His defense. The trust of our people in God should be declared on our national coins."*

Those words were not symbolic—they were confessional. In 1864, *In God We Trust* first appeared on a two-cent coin. It was not a political statement, but a national acknowledgment that America's hope did not rest solely in armies, wealth, or leaders, but in God Himself.

BECOMING THE NATIONAL MOTTO

Though the phrase appeared on various coins throughout the late nineteenth and early twentieth centuries, it was not until 1956 that *In God We Trust* was officially adopted as the national motto of the United States.

This decision came during the Cold War, when America stood in direct opposition to atheistic communism. Once again, the nation publicly affirmed what it had always believed—that freedom flows from faith, and liberty depends upon moral truth.

The following year, the motto was added to paper currency, where it remains today.

This was not the introduction of a new belief, but the formal recognition of one that had existed since our founding.

Today, *In God We Trust* is inscribed or displayed in

countless places: on U.S. coins and paper currency, inside the U.S. Capitol and other federal buildings, in courtrooms and legislative chambers, on monuments, memorials, and public displays across the nation

These inscriptions serve as quiet reminders of a truth Americans once spoke openly and without hesitation.

MORE THAN A CATCHPHRASE

In God We Trust is not a slogan meant to divide, nor a relic of a bygone era. It is a declaration of humility. It acknowledges that liberty is fragile, that power is limited, and that human government is insufficient on its own.

From the earliest days of America, our leaders understood this. The Declaration of Independence appeals to the *"Laws of Nature and of Nature's God."* The Founders repeatedly spoke of Providence, divine favor, and moral accountability. George Washington warned that national morality could not be sustained without religious principle. John Adams stated plainly that the Constitution was made for a moral and religious people.

They understood what history has proven time and again: freedom cannot survive without virtue, and virtue cannot endure without a firm reliance upon, and faith in God.

Scripture affirms this truth: *"Righteousness exalteth a nation: but sin is a reproach to any people"* (Proverbs 14:34).

To trust in God is not to abandon responsibility—it is to recognize where ultimate authority lies. It is to govern, labor, fight, and live with the understanding that we are accountable to something higher than ourselves.

In God We Trust is woven into the fabric of American identity because dependence upon God was woven into the American experiment itself. When we remember that truth, we remember who we are—and why this nation exists at all.

E Pluribus Unum
Out of Many, One

E Pluribus Unum—Latin for "Out of many, one"—captures a simple but radical idea: that a single nation could be formed from many people, many colonies, and many backgrounds without erasing their differences.

The phrase did not originate in government halls. It had been used for years in popular writings and publications in the American colonies, often to describe unity formed from diversity. By the time of the American Revolution, it already carried meaning. Thirteen separate colonies, each with its own character, customs, and interests, were choosing to stand together.

In 1776, as the colonies declared their independence from Great Britain, Congress appointed a committee to design a national seal. Among those involved were Benjamin Franklin, John Adams, and Thomas Jefferson. Over the next several years, multiple designs were proposed, revised, and rejected. During this process, *E Pluribus Unum* consistently appeared as a guiding idea.

When the Great Seal of the United States was finally approved in 1782, the motto found its place. It appears on a ribbon held in the beak of the bald eagle. The shield on the eagle's chest displays thirteen stripes, representing the original states, bound together as one. The olive branch and arrows in its talons symbolize peace and strength—both held by a united nation.

E Pluribus Unum was never meant to suggest uniformity. The founders understood that Americans would differ in beliefs, backgrounds, and opinions. Unity was not achieved by sameness, but by shared principles—liberty, self-government, and the rule of law.

For generations, the motto served as an unofficial creed of the United States. It appeared on coins, official documents, and public buildings, reminding Americans that their strength did not come from any single state, person, or group, but from their willingness to stand together.

Out of many—one nation. One people. One shared responsibility to preserve the union they inherited.

God Save the Flag

Oliver Wendell Holmes

Washed in the blood of the brave and the blooming,
Snatched from the altars of insolent foes,
Burning with star-fires, but never consuming,
Flash its broad ribbons of lily and rose.

Vainly the prophets of Baal would rend it,
Vainly his worshippers pray for its fall;
Thousands have died for it, millions defend it,
Emblem of justice and mercy to all;

Justice that reddens the sky with her terrors,
Mercy that comes with her white-handed train,
Soothing all passions, redeeming all errors,
Sheathing the sabre and breaking the chain.

Borne on the deluge of all usurpations,
Drifted our Ark o'er the desolate seas,
Bearing the rainbow of hope to the nations,
Torn from the storm-cloud and flung to the breeze!

God bless the Flag and its loyal defenders,
While its broad folds o'er the battle-field wave,
Till the dim star-wreath rekindle its splendors,
Washed from its stains in the blood of the brave.

God, Give Us Men!
Josiah Gilbert Holland

GOD, give us men!
A time like this demands
Strong minds, great hearts, true faith and ready hands;
Men whom the lust of office does not kill;
Men whom the spoils of office can not buy;
Men who possess opinions and a will;
Men who have honor; men who will not lie;
Men who can stand before a demagogue
And damn his treacherous flatteries without winking!
Tall men, sun-crowned, who live above the fog
In public duty, and in private thinking;
For while the rabble, with their thumb-worn creeds,
Their large professions and their little deeds,
Mingle in selfish strife, lo! Freedom weeps,
Wrong rules the land and waiting Justice sleeps.

Centennial Hymn

John Greenleaf Whittier

Our fathers' God! from out whose hand
The centuries fall like grains of sand,
We meet to-day, united, free,
And loyal to our land and Thee,
To thank Thee for the era done,
And trust Thee for the opening one.

Here, where of old, by Thy design,
The fathers spake that word of Thine
Whose echo is the glad refrain
Of rended bolt and falling chain,
To grace our festal time, from all
The zones of earth our guests we call.

Be with us while the New World greets
The Old World thronging all its streets,
Unveiling all the triumphs won
By art or toil beneath the sun;
And unto common good ordain
This rivalship of hand and brain.

Thou, who hast here in concord furled
The war flags of a gathered world,
Beneath our Western skies fulfil
The Orient's mission of good-will,

And, freighted with love's Golden Fleece,
Send back its Argonauts of peace.

For art and labor met in truce,
For beauty made the bride of use,
We thank Thee; but, withal, we crave
The austere virtues strong to save,
The honor proof to place or gold,
The manhood never bought nor sold.

Oh make Thou us, through centuries long,
In peace secure, in justice strong;
Around our gift of freedom draw
The safeguards of Thy righteous law
And, cast in some diviner mould,
Let the new cycle shame the old!

Part Two

THE ARCHITECTURE OF FREEDOM

How freedom is defined and protected

Introduction to
The Declaration of Independence

THE BIRTH OF THE UNITED STATES

In the early days of the American Revolution, the majority of American colonists had no wish to separate from England. They revolted against the government of King George III because they believed he was denying them their just rights as loyal British subjects. They sent him petitions, respectfully asking for a redress of their wrongs, but George III answered only with troops and ships to put down the rebellion.

"The king has plundered our seas, ravaged our coasts, burnt our towns and destroyed our people," said Thomas Jefferson, who foresaw that a complete break with the monarchy of England was the only way in which the colonies could solve their problems.

THE DECISION FOR INDEPENDENCE

In January, 1776, Thomas Paine advocated independence in his famous pamphlet, "Common Sense."

That pamphlet sold one hundred thousand copies, and throughout the colonies the people were thrilled by his dramatic appeal: "Here is the vast continent of North America, suited to become the home of a race of free men; let it no longer lie at the feet of an unworthy king."

The following June, when the second Continental Congress was meeting in Philadelphia, Richard Henry Lee of Virginia made a motion: "That these United States are, and of right ought to be, free and independent states..." and it was decided that the motion should be voted upon the next month.

THE BIRTHDAY OF A NEW DEMOCRACY

A committee was appointed to draw up a Declaration. Thomas Jefferson wrote the first draft, John Adams and Benjamin Franklin made suggestions, and the revised draft was submitted to the Continental Congress. On the fourth of July, 1776—our country's birthday—it was adopted, and the Liberty Bell in the belfry of the State House rang out the glad news to all the people of Philadelphia. They shouted with joy, cannon were fired, and the streets echoed the sounds of celebration. Riders on swift horses dashed off to carry the glorious news to the far corners of the colonies.

For, though people realized the colonies would not actually be independent until they won the war, they now felt they were fighting in a great cause. John Adams was expressing the feeling of thousands of patriots when he wrote: "Yesterday the greatest question was decided which ever was debated in America; a greater perhaps never was, nor will be, decided among men..."

THE AUTHOR OF THE DECLARATION

Thomas Jefferson wrote the Declaration of Independence.

He was extremely well fitted for the task. Though only thirty-three years old at the time, he was a thorough scholar, familiar with the writings of the great liberal thinkers who advocated greater freedom for the individual. The Declaration not only stated that the colonies were separating from the mother country but advocated a new theory of government, a new way of life. The idea that a government has certain definite obligations and the individual certain definite rights did not originate with Thomas Jefferson, but he clothed it in such simple, beautiful prose that he made it understandable to the average person. He was able to present this idea with peculiar force, for he had grown up near the frontier and had a healthy respect for the frontiersman's ability to govern himself. He believed with all his heart that this privilege should be extended to all men.

"I never had a feeling politically that did not spring from the sentiments in the Declaration of Independence." In these words Abraham Lincoln summed up his debt to Thomas Jefferson—a debt which every patriotic American also owes.

Complete text of the
The Declaration of Independence

In Congress, July 4, 1776

The unanimous Declaration of the thirteen united States of America

The unanimous Declaration of the thirteen united States of America, When in the Course of human events, it becomes necessary for one people to dissolve the political bands which have connected them with another, and to assume among the powers of the earth, the separate and equal station to which the Laws of Nature and of Nature's God entitle them, a decent respect to the opinions of mankind requires that they should declare the causes which impel them to the separation.

We hold these truths to be self-evident, that all men are created equal, that they are endowed by their Creator with certain unalienable Rights, that among these are Life, Liberty and the pursuit of Happiness.–That to secure these rights, Governments are instituted among Men, deriving their just powers from the consent of the governed, –That whenever any Form of Government becomes destructive of these ends, it is the Right of the People to alter or to abolish it, and to institute new Government, laying its foundation on such principles and organizing its powers in such form, as to them shall seem most likely to effect their Safety and Happiness. Prudence, indeed, will dictate that Governments long established should not be changed for light and transient causes; and accordingly all experience hath shewn, that mankind are more disposed to suffer, while evils are sufferable, than to right themselves by abolishing the forms to which they are accustomed. But when a long train of abuses and usurpations, pursuing invariably the same Object evinces a design to reduce them under absolute Despotism, it is their right, it is their duty, to throw off such Government, and to provide new Guards for their future security.—Such has been the patient sufferance of these Colonies; and such is now the necessity which constrains them to alter their former Systems of Government. The history of the present King of Great Britain is a history of repeated injuries and usurpations, all having in direct object the establishment of an absolute Tyranny over these States. To prove this, let Facts be submitted to a candid world.

He has refused his Assent to Laws, the most wholesome and necessary for the public good.

He has forbidden his Governors to pass Laws of immediate and pressing importance, unless suspended in their operation till his Assent should be obtained; and when so suspended, he has utterly neglected to attend to them.

He has refused to pass other Laws for the accommodation of large districts of people, unless those people would relinquish the right of Representation in the Legislature, a right inestimable to them and formidable to tyrants only.

He has called together legislative bodies at places unusual, uncomfortable, and distant from the depository of their public Records, for the sole purpose of fatiguing them into compliance with his measures.

He has dissolved Representative Houses repeatedly, for opposing with manly firmness his invasions on the rights of the people.

He has refused for a long time, after such dissolutions, to cause others to be elected; whereby the Legislative powers, incapable of Annihilation, have returned to the People at large for their exercise; the State remaining in the mean time exposed to all the dangers of invasion from without, and convulsions within.

He has endeavoured to prevent the population of these States; for that purpose obstructing the Laws for Naturalization of Foreigners; refusing to pass others to encourage their migrations hither, and raising the conditions of new Appropriations of Lands.

He has obstructed the Administration of Justice, by refusing his Assent to Laws for establishing Judiciary powers.

He has made Judges dependent on his Will alone, for the tenure of their offices, and the amount and payment of their salaries. He has erected a multitude of New Offices, and sent hither swarms of Officers to harrass our people, and eat out their substance.

He has kept among us, in times of peace, Standing Armies without the Consent of our legislatures.

He has affected to render the Military independent of and superior to the Civil power.

He has combined with others to subject us to a jurisdiction

foreign to our constitution, and unacknowledged by our laws; giving his Assent to their Acts of pretended Legislation:

For Quartering large bodies of armed troops among us:

For protecting them, by a mock Trial, from punishment for any Murders which they should commit on the Inhabitants of these States:

For cutting off our Trade with all parts of the world: For imposing Taxes on us without our Consent:

For depriving us in many cases, of the benefits of Trial by Jury:

For transporting us beyond Seas to be tried for pretended offences

For abolishing the free System of English Laws in a neighbouring Province, establishing therein an Arbitrary government, and enlarging its Boundaries so as to render it at once an example and fit instrument for introducing the same absolute rule into these Colonies:

For taking away our Charters, abolishing our most valuable Laws, and altering fundamentally the Forms of our Governments:

For suspending our own Legislatures, and declaring themselves invested with power to legislate for us in all cases whatsoever.

He has abdicated Government here, by declaring us out of his Protection and waging War against us.

He has plundered our seas, ravaged our Coasts, burnt our towns, and destroyed the lives of our people.

He is at this time transporting large Armies of foreign Mercenaries to compleat the works of death, desolation and tyranny, already begun with circumstances of Cruelty & perfidy scarcely paralleled in the most barbarous ages, and totally unworthy the Head of a civilized nation.

He has constrained our fellow Citizens taken Captive on the high Seas to bear Arms against their Country, to become the executioners of their friends and Brethren, or to fall themselves by their Hands.

He has excited domestic insurrections amongst us, and has endeavoured to bring on the inhabitants of our frontiers, the merciless Indian Savages, whose known rule of warfare, is an undistinguished destruction of all ages, sexes and conditions.

In every stage of these Oppressions We have Petitioned for Redress in the most humble terms: Our repeated Petitions have been answered only by repeated injury. A Prince whose character is thus marked by every act which may define a Tyrant, is unfit to be the ruler of a free people.

Nor have We been wanting in attentions to our Brittish brethren. We have warned them from time to time of attempts by their legislature to extend an unwarrantable jurisdiction over us. We have reminded them of the circumstances of our emigration and settlement here. We have appealed to their native justice and magnanimity, and we have conjured them by the ties of our common kindred to disavow these usurpations, which, would inevitably interrupt our connections and correspondence. They too have been deaf to the voice of justice and of consanguinity. We must, therefore, acquiesce in the necessity, which denounces our Separation, and hold them, as we hold the rest of mankind, Enemies in War, in Peace Friends.

We, therefore, the Representatives of the united States of America, in General Congress, Assembled, appealing to the Supreme Judge of the world for the rectitude of our intentions, do, in the Name, and by Authority of the good People of these Colonies, solemnly publish and declare, That these United Colonies are, and of Right ought to be Free and Independent States; that they are Absolved from all Allegiance to the British Crown, and that all political connection between them and the State of Great Britain, is and ought to be totally dissolved; and that as Free and Independent States, they have full Power to levy War, conclude Peace, contract Alliances, establish Commerce, and to do all other Acts and Things which Independent States may of right do. And for the support of this Declaration, with a firm reliance on the protection of divine Providence, we mutually pledge to each other our Lives, our Fortunes and our sacred Honor.

SIGNERS OF THE DECLARATION

New Hampshire:
Josiah Bartlett, William Whipple, Matthew Thornton

Massachusetts:
John Hancock, Samuel Adams, John Adams, Robert Treat Paine, Elbridge Gerry

Rhode Island:
Stephen Hopkins, William Ellery

Connecticut:
Roger Sherman, Samuel Huntington, William Williams, Oliver Wolcott

New York:
William Floyd, Philip Livingston, Francis Lewis, Lewis Morris

New Jersey:
Richard Stockton, John Witherspoon, Francis Hopkinson, John Hart, Abraham Clark

Pennsylvania:
Robert Morris, Benjamin Rush, Benjamin Franklin, John Morton, George Clymer, James Smith, George Taylor, James Wilson, George Ross

Delaware:
Caesar Rodney, George Read, Thomas McKean

Maryland:
Samuel Chase, William Paca, Thomas Stone, Charles Carroll of Carrollton

Virginia:
George Wythe, Richard Henry Lee, Thomas Jefferson, Benjamin Harrison, Thomas Nelson, Jr., Francis Lightfoot Lee, Carter Braxton

North Carolina:
William Hooper, Joseph Hewes, John Penn

South Carolina:
Edward Rutledge, Thomas Heyward, Jr., Thomas Lynch, Jr., Arthur Middleton

Georgia:
Button Gwinnett, Lyman Hall, George Walton

Introduction to
The Constitution

The thirteen colonies won their fight to be free and independent states. The mother country recognized their independence, but peace brought new dangers. As one historian said, "We were like a barrel made of thirteen stout staves, but yet without a single hoop to hold together." Now that they faced no common danger, colonies had begun quarreling bitterly among themselves. The country was greatly in debt, and business seemed at a standstill.

THE ARTICLES OF CONFEDERATION

The reason for this was that the central government was very inefficient. In 1778, the Continental Congress had adopted the Articles of Confederation, but this provided for a mere "league of friendship" among the states. There was no head to the government and no Supreme Court and, although there was a Congress, it had no power to enforce the laws it passed or to collect taxes.

It soon became apparent to leaders like George Washington that if the new nation was to survive it must have a much stronger central government. It must have a government that would solve the problems, not just of the individual states, but of the country as a whole. In the spring of 1787 a

Constitutional Convention was assembled in Philadelphia, in the same State House (now Independence Hall) where the Declaration of Independence had been signed.

THE CONSTITUTIONAL CONVENTION

Among the fifty-five delegates to that Convention were some of the ablest men of the day, James Madison, sometimes called the Father of the Constitution; Benjamin Franklin, Alexander Hamilton and Robert Morris. By a unanimous vote Washington was elected president. During the stormy sessions in the following weeks, he presided in a chair with a picture of the sun painted on the back.

"I could never determine whether it was a rising or a setting sun," said Benjamin Franklin afterward, remembering how close the Constitutional Convention had come to failure.

For the delegates had many difficult problems to solve. They wisely decided to adopt a new Constitution, rather than try to amend the old Articles of Confederation, but they disagreed on many points. One faction, led by Alexander Hamilton, wanted a strong centralized government, with the individual states subordinate to it. Another faction, fearing that such a government might some day become so strong as to oppress the people, wanted a decentralized system with the individual states retaining the supreme power.

Another disagreement arose between the delegates from the larger and the smaller states. The larger states wanted representation in Congress to be determined by population. The smaller states, fearing that the larger states might be able to outvote them, demanded that each state, regardless of size, be allowed an equal number of representatives. Finally a compromise was agreed upon. It provided that Congress was to consist of two houses: a House of Representatives in which states should be represented according to their population, and a Senate to which each state large and small alike, should send two members.

That was only one of a number of compromises. During the hot summer months in the old State House, there were many heated debates behind locked doors, as the delegates ironed out one difficulty after another. Finally in September a committee headed by Gouverneur Morris submitted a draft of the proposed Constitution and, a few days later, a revised draft, which was signed by thirty-nine of the fifty-five delegates. Glancing at the sun painted on the back of Washington's chair, Benjamin Franklin said, "Now I am satisfied: it is a rising sun." William Gladstone, the great English statesman, called the Constitution "the most wonderful work ever struck off at a given time by the brain and purpose of man."

THE NEW GOVERNMENT

The Constitution provided that it should go into effect after nine states had ratified it. By the following June, nine states had signified their approval, and the old Congress made plans for putting the new government into operation. George Washington was unanimously elected the first President of the United States, and on April 30, 1789, he arrived in New York, our nation's first capital, to take the oath of office.

THE BILL OF RIGHTS

The Constitution was ratified by some of the states on the

condition that certain amendments be added to guarantee their rights as individuals against any encroachment by the Federal government. Accordingly, the first Congress passed a number of amendments, ten of which were ratified by three-fourths of the state legislatures in accordance with the provisions of the Constitution itself.

These ten amendments became a part of the Constitution on December 15, 1791, and are known as the Bill of Rights. They guarantee freedom of religious worship, freedom of speech and of the press, the right to petition the government for redress of wrongs, the right to keep and bear arms, immunity from enforced quartering of soldiers, security against search and seizure without warrant, inviolability against being imprisoned without indictment and against being twice tried for the same offense and against being punished (deprived of life, liberty, or property) without due process of law, the right to to prompt trial by jury, and the prohibition of severe fines or cruel punishment.

The ninth amendment reserves to the people all rights not expressly delegated by the Constitution, and the tenth reserves to the states such powers as are not delegated to the Federal Government.

MORE RECENT AMENDMENTS

In Article V the Constitution made provision for amending the Constitution from time to time as need should arise. In addition to the Bill of Rights, seventeen other Amendments to the Constitution have been passed, modifying some of the original provisions with respect to judicial powers, elections and suffrage, abolition of slavery, income tax, and terms of office.

Complete text of the
The Constitution of the United States of America

PREAMBLE

We the People of the United States, in Order to form a more perfect Union, establish Justice, insure domestic Tranquility, provide for the common defence, promote the general Welfare, and secure the Blessings of Liberty to ourselves and our Posterity, do ordain and establish this Constitution for the United States of America.

Article. I. The Legislative Branch

Section. 1.

All legislative Powers herein granted shall be vested in a Congress of the United States, which shall consist of a Senate and House of Representatives.

The House of Representatives
Section. 2.

The House of Representatives shall be composed of Members chosen every second Year by the People of the several States, and the Electors in each State shall have the Qualifications requisite for Electors of the most numerous Branch of the State Legislature.

No Person shall be a Representative who shall not have attained to the Age of twenty five Years, and been seven Years a Citizen of the United States, and who shall not, when elected, be an Inhabitant of that State in which he shall be chosen.

Representatives and direct Taxes shall be apportioned among the several States which may be included within this Union, according to their respective Numbers, which shall be determined by adding to the whole Number of free Persons, including those bound to Service for a Term of Years, and excluding Indians not taxed, three fifths of all other Persons. The actual Enumeration shall be made within three Years after the first Meeting of the Congress of the United States, and within every subsequent Term of ten Years, in such Manner as they shall by Law direct. The Number of Representatives shall not exceed one for every thirty Thousand, but each State shall have at Least one Representative; and until such enumeration shall be made, the State of New Hampshire shall be entitled to chuse three, Massachusetts eight, Rhode-Island and Providence Plantations one, Connecticut five, New-York six, New Jersey four, Pennsylvania eight, Delaware one, Maryland six, Virginia ten, North Carolina five, South Carolina five, and Georgia three.
[Later modified by Amendment XIII and XIV]

When vacancies happen in the Representation from any State, the Executive Authority thereof shall issue Writs of Election to fill such Vacancies.

The House of Representatives shall chuse their Speaker and other Officers; and shall have the sole Power of Impeachment.

The Senate
Section. 3.

The Senate of the United States shall be composed of two Senators from each State, chosen by the Legislature thereof, for six Years; and each Senator shall have one Vote.
[Later modified by Amendment XVII]

Immediately after they shall be assembled in Consequence of the first Election, they shall be divided as equally as may be into three Classes. The Seats of the Senators of the first Class shall be vacated at the Expiration of the second Year, of the second Class at the Expiration of the fourth Year, and of the third Class at the Expiration of the sixth Year, so that one third may be chosen every second Year; and if Vacancies happen by Resignation, or otherwise, during the Recess of the Legislature of any State, the Executive thereof may make temporary Appointments until the next Meeting of the Legislature, which shall then fill such Vacancies.
[Later modified by Amendment XVII]

No Person shall be a Senator who shall not have attained to the Age of thirty Years, and been nine Years a Citizen of the United States, and who shall not, when elected, be an Inhabitant of that State for which he shall be chosen.

The Vice President of the United States shall be President of the Senate, but shall have no Vote, unless they be equally divided.

The Senate shall chuse their other Officers, and also

a President pro tempore, in the Absence of the Vice President, or when he shall exercise the Office of President of the United States.

The Senate shall have the sole Power to try all Impeachments. When sitting for that Purpose, they shall be on Oath or Affirmation. When the President of the United States is tried, the Chief Justice shall preside: And no Person shall be convicted without the Concurrence of two thirds of the Members present.

Judgment in Cases of Impeachment shall not extend further than to removal from Office, and disqualification to hold and enjoy any Office of honor, Trust or Profit under the United States: but the Party convicted shall nevertheless be liable and subject to Indictment, Trial, Judgment and Punishment, according to Law.

Elections
Section. 4.

The Times, Places and Manner of holding Elections for Senators and Representatives, shall be prescribed in each State by the Legislature thereof; but the Congress may at any time by Law make or alter such Regulations, except as to the Places of chusing Senators.

The Congress shall assemble at least once in every Year, and such Meeting shall be on the first Monday in December, unless they shall by Law appoint a different Day.
[Later modified by Amendment XX]

Powers and Duties of Congress
Section. 5.

Each House shall be the Judge of the Elections, Returns and Qualifications of its own Members, and a Majority of each shall constitute a Quorum to do Business; but a smaller Number may adjourn from day to day, and may be authorized to compel the Attendance of absent Members, in such Manner, and under such Penalties as each House may provide.

Each House may determine the Rules of its Proceedings, punish its Members for disorderly Behaviour, and, with the Concurrence of two thirds, expel a Member.

Each House shall keep a Journal of its Proceedings, and from time to time publish the same, excepting such Parts as may in their Judgment require Secrecy; and the Yeas and Nays of the Members of either House on any question shall, at the Desire of one fifth of those Present, be entered on the Journal.

Neither House, during the Session of Congress, shall, without the Consent of the other, adjourn for more than three days, nor to any other Place than that in which the two Houses shall be sitting.

Rights and Disabilities of Members
Section. 6.

The Senators and Representatives shall receive a Compensation for their Services, to be ascertained by Law, and paid out of the Treasury of the United States. They shall in all Cases, except Treason, Felony and Breach of the Peace, be privileged from Arrest during their Attendance at the Session of their respective Houses, and in going to and returning from the same; and for any Speech or Debate in either House, they shall not be questioned in any other Place.

No Senator or Representative shall, during the Time for which he was elected, be appointed to any civil Office under the Authority of the United States, which shall have been created, or the Emoluments whereof shall have been encreased during such time; and no Person holding any Office under the United States, shall be a Member of either House during his Continuance in Office.

Legislative Process
Section. 7.

All Bills for raising Revenue shall originate in the House of Representatives; but the Senate may propose or concur with Amendments as on other Bills.

Every Bill which shall have passed the House of Representatives and the Senate, shall, before it become a Law, be presented to the President of the United States; If he approve he shall sign it, but if not he shall return it, with his Objections to that House in which it shall have originated, who shall enter the Objections at large on their Journal, and proceed to reconsider it. If after such Reconsideration two thirds of that House shall agree to pass the Bill, it shall be sent, together with the Objections, to the other House, by which it shall likewise be reconsidered, and if approved by two thirds of that House, it shall become a Law. But in all such Cases the Votes of both Houses shall be determined by yeas and Nays, and the Names of the Persons voting for and against the Bill shall be entered on the Journal of each House respectively. If any Bill shall not be returned by the President within ten Days (Sundays excepted) after it shall have been presented to him, the Same shall be a Law, in like Manner as if he had signed it, unless the Congress by their Adjournment prevent its Return, in which Case it shall not be a Law.

Every Order, Resolution, or Vote to which the Concurrence of the Senate and House of Representatives may be necessary (except on a question of Adjournment) shall be presented to the President of the United States; and before the Same shall take Effect, shall be approved by him, or being disapproved by him, shall be repassed by two thirds of the Senate and House of Representatives, according to the Rules and Limitations prescribed in the Case of a Bill.

Powers of Congress
Section. 8.

The Congress shall have Power To lay and collect Taxes, Duties, Imposts and Excises, to pay the Debts and provide for the common Defence and general Welfare of the United States; but all Duties, Imposts and Excises shall be uniform throughout the United States;

To borrow Money on the credit of the United States;

To regulate Commerce with foreign Nations, and among the several States, and with the Indian Tribes;

To establish an uniform Rule of Naturalization, and uniform Laws on the subject of Bankruptcies throughout the United States;

To coin Money, regulate the Value thereof, and of foreign Coin, and fix the Standard of Weights and Measures;

To provide for the Punishment of counterfeiting the Securities and current Coin of the United States;

To establish Post Offices and post Roads;

To promote the Progress of Science and useful Arts, by securing for limited Times to Authors and Inventors the exclusive Right to their respective Writings and Discoveries;

To constitute Tribunals inferior to the supreme Court;

To define and punish Piracies and Felonies committed on the high Seas, and Offences against the Law of Nations;

To declare War, grant Letters of Marque and Reprisal, and make Rules concerning Captures on Land and Water;

To raise and support Armies, but no Appropriation of Money to that Use shall be for a longer Term than two Years;

To provide and maintain a Navy;

To make Rules for the Government and Regulation of the land and naval Forces;

To provide for calling forth the Militia to execute the Laws of the Union, suppress Insurrections and repel Invasions;

To provide for organizing, arming, and disciplining, the Militia, and for governing such Part of them as may be employed in the Service of the United States, reserving to the States respectively, the Appointment of the Officers, and the Authority of training the Militia according to the discipline prescribed by Congress;

To exercise exclusive Legislation in all Cases whatsoever, over such District (not exceeding ten Miles square) as may, by Cession of particular States, and the Acceptance of Congress, become the Seat of the Government of the United States, and to exercise like Authority over all Places purchased by the Consent of the Legislature of the State in which the Same shall be, for the Erection of Forts, Magazines, Arsenals, dock-Yards, and other needful Buildings;—And

To make all Laws which shall be necessary and proper for carrying into Execution the foregoing Powers, and all other Powers vested by this Constitution in the Government of the United States, or in any Department or Officer thereof.

Powers Denied Congress
Section. 9.

The Migration or Importation of such Persons as any of the States now existing shall think proper to admit, shall not be prohibited by the Congress prior to the Year one thousand eight hundred and eight, but a Tax or duty may be imposed on such Importation, not exceeding ten dollars for each Person.

The Privilege of the Writ of Habeas Corpus shall not be suspended, unless when in Cases of Rebellion or Invasion the public Safety may require it.

No Bill of Attainder or ex post facto Law shall be passed.

No Capitation, or other direct, Tax shall be laid, unless in Proportion to the Census or enumeration herein before directed to be taken.
[Superseded by Amendment XVI]

No Tax or Duty shall be laid on Articles exported from any State.

No Preference shall be given by any Regulation of Commerce or Revenue to the Ports of one State over those of another: nor shall Vessels bound to, or from, one State, be obliged to enter, clear, or pay Duties in another.

No Money shall be drawn from the Treasury, but in Consequence of Appropriations made by Law; and a regular Statement and Account of the Receipts and Expenditures of all public Money shall be published from time to time.

No Title of Nobility shall be granted by the United States: And no Person holding any Office of Profit or Trust under them, shall, without the Consent of the Congress, accept of any present, Emolument, Office, or Title, of any kind whatever, from any King, Prince, or foreign State.

Powers Denied to the States
Section. 10.

No State shall enter into any Treaty, Alliance, or Confederation; grant Letters of Marque and Reprisal; coin Money; emit Bills of Credit; make any Thing but gold and silver Coin a Tender in Payment of Debts; pass any Bill of Attainder, ex post facto Law, or Law impairing the Obligation of Contracts, or grant any Title of Nobility.

No State shall, without the Consent of the Congress, lay any Imposts or Duties on Imports or Exports, except what may be absolutely necessary for executing it's inspection Laws: and the net Produce of all Duties and Imposts, laid by any State on Imports or Exports, shall be for the Use of the Treasury of the United States; and all such Laws shall be subject to the Revision and Controul of the Congress.

No State shall, without the Consent of Congress, lay any Duty of Tonnage, keep Troops, or Ships of War in time of Peace, enter into any Agreement or Compact with another State, or with a foreign Power, or engage in War, unless actually invaded, or in such imminent Danger as will not admit of delay.

Article. II. The Executive Branch

President and Vice-President
Section. 1.

The executive Power shall be vested in a President of the United States of America. He shall hold his Office during the Term of four Years, and, together with the Vice President, chosen for the same Term, be elected, as follows

Each State shall appoint, in such Manner as the Legislature thereof may direct, a Number of Electors, equal to the whole Number of Senators and Representatives to which the State may be entitled in the Congress: but no Senator or Representative, or Person holding an Office of Trust or Profit under the United States, shall be appointed an Elector.

The Electors shall meet in their respective States, and vote by Ballot for two Persons, of whom one at least shall not be an Inhabitant of the same State with themselves. And they shall make a List of all the Persons voted for, and of the Number of Votes for each; which List they shall sign and certify, and transmit sealed to the Seat of the Government of the United States, directed to the President of the Senate. The President of the Senate shall, in the

Presence of the Senate and House of Representatives, open all the Certificates, and the Votes shall then be counted. The Person having the greatest Number of Votes shall be the President, if such Number be a Majority of the whole Number of Electors appointed; and if there be more than one who have such Majority, and have an equal Number of Votes, then the House of Representatives shall immediately chuse by Ballot one of them for President; and if no Person have a Majority, then from the five highest on the List the said House shall in like Manner chuse the President. But in chusing the President, the Votes shall be taken by States, the Representation from each State having one Vote; A quorum for this Purpose shall consist of a Member or Members from two thirds of the States, and a Majority of all the States shall be necessary to a Choice. In every Case, after the Choice of the President, the Person having the greatest Number of Votes of the Electors shall be the Vice President. But if there should remain two or more who have equal Votes, the Senate shall chuse from them by Ballot the Vice President.

[Superseded by Amendments XII and XX]

The Congress may determine the Time of chusing the Electors, and the Day on which they shall give their Votes; which Day shall be the same throughout the United States.

Who May Become President?

No Person except a natural born Citizen, or a Citizen of the United States, at the time of the Adoption of this Constitution, shall be eligible to the Office of President; neither shall any Person be eligible to that Office who shall not have attained to the Age of thirty five Years, and been fourteen Years a Resident within the United States.

In Case of the Removal of the President from Office, or of his Death, Resignation, or Inability to discharge the Powers and Duties of the said Office, the Same shall devolve on the Vice President, and the Congress may by Law provide for the Case of Removal, Death, Resignation or Inability, both of the President and Vice President, declaring what Officer shall then act as President, and such Officer shall act accordingly, until the Disability be removed, or a President shall be elected.
[Superseded by Amendment XXV]

The President shall, at stated Times, receive for his Services, a Compensation, which shall neither be encreased nor diminished during the Period for which he shall have been elected, and he shall not receive within that Period any other Emolument from the United States, or any of them.

President's Oath of Office

Before he enter on the Execution of his Office, he shall take the following Oath or Affirmation:—"I do solemnly swear (or affirm) that I will faithfully execute the Office of President of the United States, and will to the best of my Ability, preserve, protect and defend the Constitution of the United States."

Duties and Powers of the President
Section. 2.

The President shall be Commander in Chief of the Army and Navy of the United States, and of the Militia of the several States, when called into the actual Service of the United States; he may require the Opinion, in writing, of the principal Officer in each of the executive Departments, upon any Subject relating to the Duties of their respective

Offices, and he shall have Power to grant Reprieves and Pardons for Offences against the United States, except in Cases of Impeachment.

He shall have Power, by and with the Advice and Consent of the Senate, to make Treaties, provided two thirds of the Senators present concur; and he shall nominate, and by and with the Advice and Consent of the Senate, shall appoint Ambassadors, other public Ministers and Consuls, Judges of the supreme Court, and all other Officers of the United States, whose Appointments are not herein otherwise provided for, and which shall be established by Law: but the Congress may by Law vest the Appointment of such inferior Officers, as they think proper, in the President alone, in the Courts of Law, or in the Heads of Departments.

The President shall have Power to fill up all Vacancies that may happen during the Recess of the Senate, by granting Commissions which shall expire at the End of their next Session.

Section. 3.

He shall from time to time give to the Congress Information of the State of the Union, and recommend to their Consideration such Measures as he shall judge necessary and expedient; he may, on extraordinary Occasions, convene both Houses, or either of them, and in Case of Disagreement between them, with Respect to the Time of Adjournment, he may adjourn them to such Time as he shall think proper; he shall receive Ambassadors and other public Ministers; he shall take Care that the Laws be faithfully executed, and shall Commission all the Officers of the United States.

Impeaching Executive Officers
Section. 4.

The President, Vice President and all civil Officers of the United States, shall be removed from Office on Impeachment for, and Conviction of, Treason, Bribery, or other high Crimes and Misdemeanors.

Article. III. The Judicial Branch

Section. 1.

The judicial Power of the United States, shall be vested in one supreme Court, and in such inferior Courts as the Congress may from time to time ordain and establish. The Judges, both of the supreme and inferior Courts, shall hold their Offices during good Behaviour, and shall, at stated Times, receive for their Services, a Compensation, which shall not be diminished during their Continuance in Office.

Section. 2.

The judicial Power shall extend to all Cases, in Law and Equity, arising under this Constitution, the Laws of the United States, and Treaties made, or which shall be made, under their Authority;—to all Cases affecting Ambassadors, other public Ministers and Consuls;—to all Cases of admiralty and maritime Jurisdiction;—to Controversies to which the United States shall be a Party;—to Controversies between two or more States;— between a State and Citizens of another State,—between Citizens of different States,— between Citizens of the same State claiming Lands under Grants of different States, and between a State, or the Citizens thereof, and foreign States, Citizens or Subjects.
[Modified by Amendment XI]

Jurisdiction of Supreme Court

In all Cases affecting Ambassadors, other public Ministers and Consuls, and those in which a State shall be Party, the supreme Court shall have original Jurisdiction. In all the other Cases before mentioned, the supreme Court shall have appellate Jurisdiction, both as to Law and Fact, with such Exceptions, and under such Regulations as the Congress shall make.

Trial by Jury

The Trial of all Crimes, except in Cases of Impeachment, shall be by Jury; and such Trial shall be held in the State where the said Crimes shall have been committed; but when not committed within any State, the Trial shall be at such Place or Places as the Congress may by Law have directed.

Section. 3.

Treason against the United States, shall consist only in levying War against them, or in adhering to their Enemies, giving them Aid and Comfort. No Person shall be convicted of Treason unless on the Testimony of two Witnesses to the same overt Act, or on Confession in open Court.

The Congress shall have Power to declare the Punishment of Treason, but no Attainder of Treason shall work Corruption of Blood, or Forfeiture except during the Life of the Person attainted.

Article. IV. The Federal and State Governments

Their Relationship
Section. 1.

Full Faith and Credit shall be given in each State to the public Acts, Records, and judicial Proceedings of every other State. And the Congress may by general Laws prescribe the Manner in which such Acts, Records and Proceedings shall be proved, and the Effect thereof.

Section. 2.

The Citizens of each State shall be entitled to all Privileges and Immunities of Citizens in the several States.

A Person charged in any State with Treason, Felony, or other Crime, who shall flee from Justice, and be found in another State, shall on Demand of the executive Authority of the State from which he fled, be delivered up, to be removed to the State having Jurisdiction of the Crime.

No Person held to Service or Labour in one State, under the Laws thereof, escaping into another, shall, in Consequence of any Law or Regulation therein, be discharged from such Service or Labour, but shall be delivered up on Claim of the Party to whom such Service or Labour may be due.

Admitting New States
Section. 3.

New States may be admitted by the Congress into this Union; but no new State shall be formed or erected within the Jurisdiction of any other State; nor any State be formed by the Junction of two or more States, or Parts of States, without the Consent of the Legislatures of the States concerned as well as of the Congress.

The Congress shall have Power to dispose of and make all needful Rules and Regulations respecting the Territory or other Property belonging to the United States; and nothing in this Constitution shall be so construed as to Prejudice any Claims of the United States, or of any particular State.

Federal Guarantees to States
Section. 4.

The United States shall guarantee to every State in this Union a Republican Form of Government, and shall protect each of them against Invasion; and on Application of the Legislature, or of the Executive (when the Legislature cannot be convened) against domestic Violence.

Article. V. Amending The Constitution

The Congress, whenever two thirds of both Houses shall deem it necessary, shall propose Amendments to this Constitution, or, on the Application of the Legislatures of two thirds of the several States, shall call a Convention for proposing Amendments, which, in either Case, shall be valid to all Intents and Purposes, as Part of this Constitution, when ratified by the Legislatures of three fourths of the several States, or by Conventions in three fourths thereof, as the one or the other Mode of Ratification may be proposed by the Congress; Provided that no Amendment which may be made prior to the Year One thousand eight hundred and eight shall in any Manner affect the first and fourth Clauses in the Ninth Section of the first Article; and that no State, without its Consent, shall be deprived of its equal Suffrage in the Senate.

Article. VI. The Supreme Law of the Land

All Debts contracted and Engagements entered into, before the Adoption of this Constitution, shall be as valid against the United States under this Constitution, as under the Confederation.

This Constitution, and the Laws of the United States which shall be made in Pursuance thereof; and all Treaties made, or which shall be made, under the Authority of the United States, shall be the supreme Law of the Land; and the Judges in every State shall be bound thereby, any Thing in the Constitution or Laws of any State to the Contrary notwithstanding.

The Senators and Representatives before mentioned, and the Members of the several State Legislatures, and all executive and judicial Officers, both of the United States and of the several States, shall be bound by Oath or Affirmation, to support this Constitution; but no religious Test shall ever be required as a Qualification to any Office or public Trust under the United States.

Article. VII. Ratification of Constitution

The Ratification of the Conventions of nine States, shall be sufficient for the Establishment of this Constitution between the States so ratifying the Same.

AMENDMENTS TO THE CONSTITUTION

THE BILL OF RIGHTS

[The first ten Amendments, adopted in 1791, are collectively known as the "Bill of Rights."]

Amendment I
Personal Freedom

Congress shall make no law respecting an establishment of religion, or prohibiting the free exercise thereof; or abridging the freedom of speech, or of the press; or the right of the people peaceably to assemble, and to petition the Government for a redress of grievances.

Amendment II
Right to Bear Arms

A well regulated Militia, being necessary to the security of a free State, the right of the people to keep and bear Arms, shall not be infringed.

Amendment III
Quartering Soldiers

No Soldier shall, in time of peace be quartered in any house, without the consent of the Owner, nor in time of war, but in a manner to be prescribed by law.

Amendment IV
Protection Against Seizure and Search

The right of the people to be secure in their persons, houses, papers, and effects, against unreasonable searches and seizures, shall not be violated, and no Warrants shall issue, but upon probable cause, supported by Oath or affirmation, and particularly describing the place to be searched, and the persons or things to be seized.

Amendment V
Protection for Persons and Private Property

No person shall be held to answer for a capital, or otherwise infamous crime, unless on a presentment or indictment of a Grand Jury, except in cases arising in the land or naval forces, or in the Militia, when in actual service in time of War or public danger; nor shall any person be subject for the same offence to be twice put in jeopardy of life or limb; nor shall be compelled in any criminal case to be a witness against himself, nor be deprived of life, liberty, or property, without due process of law; nor shall private property be taken for public use, without just compensation.

Amendment VI
Rights of Accused Persons

In all criminal prosecutions, the accused shall enjoy the right to a speedy and public trial, by an impartial jury of the State and district wherein the crime shall have been committed, which district shall have been previously ascertained by law, and to be informed of the nature and cause of the accusation; to be confronted with the witnesses against him; to have compulsory process for obtaining witnesses in his favor, and to have the Assistance of Counsel for his defence.

Amendment VII
Trial by Jury

In Suits at common law, where the value in controversy shall exceed twenty dollars, the right of trial by jury shall be preserved, and no fact tried by a jury, shall be otherwise re-examined in any Court of the United States, than according to the rules of the common law.

Amendment VIII
Protection Against Excessive Punishments

Excessive bail shall not be required, nor excessive fines imposed, nor cruel and unusual punishments inflicted.

Amendment IX
Rights Retained by the People

The enumeration in the Constitution, of certain rights, shall not be construed to deny or disparage others retained by the people.

Amendment X
Powers Reserved to the States

The powers not delegated to the United States by the Constitution, nor prohibited by it to the States, are reserved to the States respectively, or to the people.

MORE RECENT AMENDMENTS
(With dates of adoption)

Amendment XI
Limiting Power of Federal Courts

Passed by Congress March 4, 1794. Ratified February 7, 1795.

Note: Article III, section 2, of the Constitution was modified by amendment 11.

The Judicial power of the United States shall not be construed to extend to any suit in law or equity, commenced or prosecuted against one of the United States by Citizens of another State, or by Citizens or Subjects of any Foreign State.

Amendment XII
Electoral College

Passed by Congress December 9, 1803. Ratified June 15, 1804.

Note: A portion of Article II, section 1 of the Constitution was superseded by the 12th amendment.

The Electors shall meet in their respective states and vote by ballot for President and Vice-President, one of whom, at least, shall not be an inhabitant of the same state with themselves; they shall name in their ballots the person voted for as President, and in distinct ballots the person voted for as Vice-President, and they shall make distinct lists of all persons voted for as President, and of all persons voted for as Vice-President, and of the number of votes for each, which lists they shall sign and certify, and transmit sealed to the seat of the government of the United States, directed to the President of the Senate; -- the President of the Senate shall, in the presence of the Senate and House of Representatives, open all the certificates and the votes shall then be counted; -- The person having the greatest number of votes for President, shall be the President, if such number be a majority of the whole number of Electors appointed; and if no person have such majority, then from the persons having the highest numbers not exceeding three on the list of those voted for as President, the House of Representatives shall choose immediately, by ballot, the President. But in choosing the President, the votes shall be taken by states, the representation from each state having one vote; a quorum for this purpose shall consist of a member or members from two-thirds of the states, and a majority of all the states shall be necessary to a choice. [And if the House of Representatives shall not choose a President whenever the right of choice shall devolve upon them, before the fourth day of March next following, then the Vice-President shall act as President, as in the case of the death or other constitutional disability of the President. --]* The person having the greatest number of votes as Vice-President, shall be the Vice-President, if such number be a majority of the whole number of Electors appointed, and if no person have a majority, then from the two highest numbers on the list, the Senate shall choose the Vice-President; a quorum for the purpose shall consist of two-thirds of the whole number of Senators, and a majority of the whole number shall be necessary to a choice. But no person constitutionally ineligible to the office of President shall be eligible to that of Vice-President of the United States.

*Superseded by section 3 of the 20th amendment.

Amendment XIII
Abolition of Slavery

Passed by Congress January 31, 1865. Ratified December 6, 1865.

Note: A portion of Article IV, section 2, of the Constitution was superseded by the 13th amendment.

Section 1.

Neither slavery nor involuntary servitude, except as a punishment for crime whereof the party shall have been duly convicted, shall exist within the United States, or any place subject to their jurisdiction.

Section 2.

Congress shall have power to enforce this article by appropriate legislation.

Amendment XIV

Passed by Congress June 13, 1866. Ratified July 9, 1868.

Note: Article I, section 2, of the Constitution was modified by section 2 of the 14th amendment.

Who Is A Citizen
Section 1.

All persons born or naturalized in the United States, and subject to the jurisdiction thereof, are citizens of the United States and of the State wherein they reside. No State shall make or enforce any law which shall abridge the privileges or immunities of citizens of the United States; nor shall any State deprive any person of life, liberty, or property, without due process of law; nor deny to any person within its jurisdiction the equal protection of the laws.

Representation in Congress
Section 2.

Representatives shall be apportioned among the several States according to their respective numbers, counting the whole number of persons in each State, excluding Indians not taxed. But when the right to vote at any election for the choice of electors for President and Vice-President of the United States, Representatives in Congress, the Executive and Judicial officers of a State, or the members of the Legislature thereof, is denied to any of the male inhabitants of such State, being twenty-one years of age,* and citizens of the United States, or in any way abridged, except for participation in rebellion, or other crime, the basis of representation therein shall be reduced in the proportion which the number of such male citizens shall bear to the whole number of male citizens twenty-one years of age in such State.

Section 3.

No person shall be a Senator or Representative in Congress, or elector of President and Vice-President, or hold any office, civil or military, under the United States, or under any State, who, having previously taken an oath, as a member of Congress, or as an officer of the United States, or as a member of any State legislature, or as an executive or judicial officer of any State, to support the Constitution of the United States, shall have engaged in insurrection or rebellion against the same, or given aid or comfort to the enemies thereof. But Congress may by a vote of two-thirds of each House, remove such disability.

Public Debt
Section 4.

The validity of the public debt of the United States, authorized by law, including debts incurred for payment of pensions and bounties for services in suppressing insurrection or rebellion, shall not be questioned. But neither the United States nor any State shall assume or pay any debt or obligation incurred in aid of insurrection or rebellion against the United States, or any claim for the loss or emancipation of any slave; but all such debts, obligations and claims shall be held illegal and void.

Section 5.

The Congress shall have power to enforce, by appropriate legislation, the provisions of this article.

*Changed by section 1 of the 26th amendment.

Amendment XV

Passed by Congress February 26, 1869. Ratified February 3, 1870.

Protection of Voting Rights Regardless of Race
Section 1.

The right of citizens of the United States to vote shall not be denied or abridged by the United States or by any State on account of race, color, or previous condition of servitude--

Section 2.

The Congress shall have power to enforce this article by appropriate legislation.

Amendment XVI
Federal Income Tax

Passed by Congress July 2, 1909. Ratified February 3, 1913.

Note: Article I, section 9, of the Constitution was modified by amendment 16.

The Congress shall have power to lay and collect taxes on incomes, from whatever source derived, without apportionment among the several States, and without regard to any census or enumeration.

Amendment XVII
Direct Election of U.S. Senators

Passed by Congress May 13, 1912. Ratified April 8, 1913.

Note: Article I, section 3, of the Constitution was modified by the 17th amendment.

The Senate of the United States shall be composed of two Senators from each State, elected by the people thereof, for six years; and each Senator shall have one vote. The electors in each State shall have the qualifications requisite for electors of the most numerous branch of the State legislatures.

When vacancies happen in the representation of any State in the Senate, the executive authority of such State shall issue writs of election to fill such vacancies: Provided, That the legislature of any State may empower the executive thereof to make temporary appointments until the people fill the vacancies by election as the legislature may direct.

This amendment shall not be so construed as to affect the election or term of any Senator chosen before it becomes valid as part of the Constitution.

Amendment XVIII
National Prohibition

Passed by Congress December 18, 1917. Ratified January 16, 1919. Repealed by amendment 21.

Section 1.

After one year from the ratification of this article the manufacture, sale, or transportation of intoxicating liquors within, the importation thereof into, or the exportation thereof from the United States and all territory subject to the jurisdiction thereof for beverage purposes is hereby prohibited.

Section 2.

The Congress and the several States shall have concurrent power to enforce this article by appropriate legislation.

Section 3.

This article shall be inoperative unless it shall have been ratified as an amendment to the Constitution by the legislatures of the several States, as provided in the Constitution, within seven years from the date of the submission hereof to the States by the Congress.

Amendment XIX
Women's Suffrage

Passed by Congress June 4, 1919. Ratified August 18, 1920.

The right of citizens of the United States to vote shall not be denied or abridged by the United States or by any State on account of sex.

Congress shall have power to enforce this article by appropriate legislation.

Amendment XX
Presidential and Congressional Terms

Passed by Congress March 2, 1932. Ratified January 23, 1933.

Note: Article I, section 4, of the Constitution was modified by section 2 of this amendment. In addition, a portion of the 12th amendment was superseded by section 3.

Section 1.

The terms of the President and Vice President shall end at noon on the 20th day of January, and the terms of Senators and Representatives at noon on the 3d day of January, of the years in which such terms would have ended if this article had not been ratified; and the terms of their successors shall then begin.

Section 2.

The Congress shall assemble at least once in every year, and such meeting shall begin at noon on the 3d day of January, unless they shall by law appoint a different day.

Section 3.

If, at the time fixed for the beginning of the term of the President, the President elect shall have died, the Vice President elect shall become President. If a President shall not have been chosen before the time fixed for the beginning of his term, or if the President elect shall have failed to qualify, then the Vice President elect shall act as President until a President shall have qualified; and the Congress may by law provide for the case wherein neither a President elect nor a Vice President elect shall have qualified, declaring who shall then act as President, or the manner in which one who is to act shall be selected, and such person shall act accordingly until a President or Vice President shall have qualified.

Section 4.

The Congress may by law provide for the case of the death of any of the persons from whom the House of Representatives may choose a President whenever the right of choice shall have devolved upon them, and for the case of the death of any of the persons from whom the Senate may choose a Vice President whenever the right of choice shall have devolved upon them.

Section 5.

Sections 1 and 2 shall take effect on the 15th day of October following the ratification of this article.

Section 6.

This article shall be inoperative unless it shall have been ratified as an amendment to the Constitution by the legislatures of three-fourths of the several States within seven years from the date of its submission.

Amendment XXI
Repeal of Prohibition

Passed by Congress February 20, 1933. Ratified December 5, 1933.

Section 1.

The eighteenth article of amendment to the Constitution of the United States is hereby repealed.

Section 2.

The transportation or importation into any State, Territory, or possession of the United States for delivery or use therein of intoxicating liquors, in violation of the laws thereof, is hereby prohibited.

Section 3.

This article shall be inoperative unless it shall have been ratified as an amendment to the Constitution by conventions in the several States, as provided in the Constitution, within seven years from the date of the submission hereof to the States by the Congress.

Amendment XXII
Presidential Term Limits

Passed by Congress March 21, 1947. Ratified February 27, 1951.

Section 1.

No person shall be elected to the office of the President more than twice, and no person who has held the office of President, or acted as President, for more than two years of a term to which some other person was elected President shall be elected to the office of the President more than once. But this Article shall not apply to any person holding the office of President when this Article was proposed by the Congress, and shall not prevent any person who may be holding the office of President, or acting as President, during the term within which this Article becomes operative from holding the office of President or acting as President during the remainder of such term.

Section 2.

This article shall be inoperative unless it shall have been ratified as an amendment to the Constitution by the legislatures of three-fourths of the several States within seven years from the date of its submission to the States by the Congress.

Amendment XXIII
Washington, D.C. Electoral Votes

Passed by Congress June 16, 1960. Ratified March 29, 1961.

Section 1.

The District constituting the seat of Government of the United States shall appoint in such manner as the Congress may direct:

A number of electors of President and Vice President equal to the whole number of Senators and Representatives in Congress to which the District would be entitled if it were a State, but in no event more than the least populous State; they shall be in addition to those appointed by the States, but they shall be considered, for the purposes of the election of President and Vice President, to be electors appointed by a State; and they shall meet in the District and perform such duties as provided by the twelfth article of amendment.

Section 2.

The Congress shall have power to enforce this article by appropriate legislation.

Amendment XXIV
Prohibition of Poll Taxes

Passed by Congress August 27, 1962. Ratified January 23, 1964.

Section 1.

The right of citizens of the United States to vote in any primary or other election for President or Vice President, for electors for President or Vice President, or for Senator or Representative in Congress, shall not be denied or abridged by the United States or any State by reason of failure to pay any poll tax or other tax.

Section 2.

The Congress shall have power to enforce this article by appropriate legislation.

Amendment XXV
Presidential Succession and Disability

Passed by Congress July 6, 1965. Ratified February 10, 1967.

Note: Article II, section 1, of the Constitution was affected by the 25th amendment.

Section 1.

In case of the removal of the President from office or of his death or resignation, the Vice President shall become President.

Section 2.

Whenever there is a vacancy in the office of the Vice President, the President shall nominate a Vice President who shall take office upon confirmation by a majority vote of both Houses of Congress.

Section 3.

Whenever the President transmits to the President pro tempore of the Senate and the Speaker of the House of Representatives his written declaration that he is unable to discharge the powers and duties of his office, and until he transmits to them a written declaration to the contrary, such powers and duties shall be discharged by the Vice President as Acting President.

Section 4.

Whenever the Vice President and a majority of either the principal officers of the executive departments or of such other body as Congress may by law provide, transmit to the President pro tempore of the Senate and the Speaker of the House of Representatives their written declaration that the President is unable to discharge the powers and duties of his office, the Vice President shall immediately assume the powers and duties of the office as Acting President.

Thereafter, when the President transmits to the President pro tempore of the Senate and the Speaker of the House of Representatives his written declaration that no inability exists, he shall resume the powers and duties of his office unless the Vice President and a majority of either the principal officers of the executive department or of such other body as Congress may by law provide, transmit within four days to the President pro tempore of the Senate and the Speaker of the House of Representatives their written declaration that the President is unable to discharge the powers and duties of his office. Thereupon Congress shall decide the issue, assembling within forty-eight hours for that purpose if not in session. If the Congress, within twenty-one days after receipt of the latter written declaration, or, if Congress is not in session, within twenty-one days after Congress is required to assemble, determines by two-thirds vote of both Houses that the President is unable to discharge the powers and duties of his office, the Vice President shall continue to discharge the same as Acting President; otherwise, the President shall resume the powers and duties of his office.

Amendment XXVI
Reducing the Voting Age to 18

Passed by Congress March 23, 1971. Ratified July 1, 1971.

Note: Amendment 14, section 2, of the Constitution was modified by section 1 of the 26th amendment.

Section 1.

The right of citizens of the United States, who are eighteen years of age or older, to vote shall not be denied or abridged by the United States or by any State on account of age.

Section 2.

The Congress shall have power to enforce this article by appropriate legislation.

AMENDMENT XXVII
Congressional Pay Raises

Originally proposed Sept. 25, 1789. Ratified May 7, 1992.

No law, varying the compensation for the services of the

Senators and Representatives, shall take effect, until an election of Representatives shall have intervened.

Rights And Privileges

I AM AN AMERICAN. These rights and privileges are mine:

I may think as I please.

I may speak or write as I please, so long as I do not interfere with the rights of others.

I have the right to vote. By my vote I choose the public officers who are really my servants.

I have the right to choose my work, to seek any job for which my experience and ability have fitted me.

I have the right to try to improve my lot through various means.

I have the right to a prompt trial by jury, if I should be accused of a crime.

I may seek justice in the courts, where I have equal rights with others.

I have the privilege of sharing in the benefits of many of the natural resource of my country.

I may educate my children in free schools.

I have the right to worship as I think best.

I have the right to "life, liberty and the pursuit of happiness."

I have the right to assemble peacefully and petition my government for redress of grievances.

I have the right to participate in public debate and the marketplace of ideas.

I have the right to privacy in my personal and family life.

I have the right to equal protection under the law, regardless of race, religion, gender, or background.

I have the right to access information and a free press, which keeps my government accountable.

These duties I share with my fellow citizens:

It is my duty to obey my country's laws.

It is my duty to vote, so my government may truly represent the will of the people.

It is my duty to pray for my country's leaders.

It is my duty to keep informed as to the honesty and ability of candidates for public office.

It is my duty, by my vote and influence, to correct injustice.

It is my duty to pay such taxes as have been devised by representatives elected by me, to defray the cost of government.

It is my duty to serve on juries when called on.

It is my duty to defend my country, if need should arise.

It is my duty to abide by the will of the majority, to stand behind my government, so my nation may be unified in times of crisis.

It is my duty to respect the rights and liberties of others, even when I disagree with them.

It is my duty to contribute to my community, through service, charity, and civic engagement.

It is my duty to educate myself, my family, and my neighbors about the responsibilities of citizenship.

It is my duty to uphold the Constitution and the principles of freedom, equality, and justice for all.

How Our Government Works

I AM AN AMERICAN. I am fully informed about how our Government works.

The framers of the Constitution sought to devise a system whereby the powers of government would be divided among three branches, each of which would act as a check upon the other two. Thus one branch of government would balance the others, and no one branch would be allowed to become too powerful.

THE LEGISLATIVE BRANCH

The legislative, or law-making branch, is vested in two houses of Congress: the House of Representatives and the Senate. The two houses sit separately, but the consent of both is necessary to legislation.

The House of Representatives has 435 voting members, elected for two-year terms from congressional districts in each state. Districts are apportioned based on population, with each Representative currently serving about 761,000 people.

The Senate has one hundred members, two from each state,

representing their states as a whole. Senators are elected by popular vote for six-year terms, with one-third of the Senate elected every two years to ensure continuity.

THE EXECUTIVE BRANCH

It is the duty of the President of the United States to see that laws are "faithfully executed." He recommends needed legislation to Congress, and he approves or vetoes acts passed by Congress. He is Commander-in-chief of the Armed Forces.

The Vice-President succeeds to the Presidency if the President dies or is otherwise permanently prevented from fulfilling his duties. The Vice-President has no executive powers but is the presiding officer of the Senate.

The President and Vice President are elected for four-year terms. They are chosen by electors who are selected by popular vote in each state and the District of Columbia. Each state appoints a number of electors equal to its total number of Senators and Representatives in Congress, with the District of Columbia receiving three electors.

Although the Constitution originally envisioned electors exercising independent judgment, today electors generally reflect the will of the voters and cast their ballots in accordance with the popular vote of their state, as required by law in most states.

The President's Cabinet is composed of the heads of the executive departments and serves as an advisory body to the President. Cabinet members are appointed by the President and must be confirmed by the Senate.

The Cabinet is not established by the Constitution but developed through tradition, beginning with George Washington's practice of seeking advice from department heads. Today, the Cabinet includes the Vice President and the Secretaries of State, Treasury, War, Interior, Agriculture, Commerce, Labor, Health and Human Services, Housing and Urban Development, Transportation, Energy, Education, Veterans Affairs, and Homeland Security, as well as the Attorney General.

Under the Presidential Succession Act, after the Vice President, the Speaker of the House and the President pro tempore of the Senate are next in line to the presidency. They are followed by Cabinet members in the order in which their departments were established, beginning with the Secretary of State.

THE JUDICIAL BRANCH

The Supreme Court, the highest court in the United States, plays a key role in interpreting the Constitution and determining whether laws passed by Congress or by the states are constitutional. Through the power of judicial review, the Court may declare federal or state laws unconstitutional if they conflict with the Constitution.

The Supreme Court sits in Washington, D.C. It is composed of nine Justices—one Chief Justice and eight Associate Justices—who are appointed by the President and confirmed by the Senate. Justices serve during good behavior, which effectively means for life unless they resign, retire, or are removed through impeachment.

The Supreme Court checks Congress through its power of judicial review, by which it may declare unconstitutional any law passed by Congress.

The President may recommend legislation to Congress and may veto any bill passed by Congress. A bill becomes law when it is passed by a majority of both houses of Congress and signed by the President, or if the President does not veto it within ten days while Congress is in session. Congress may override a presidential veto by a two-thirds vote of both the House of Representatives and the Senate.

The Senate must approve treaties negotiated by the President by a two-thirds vote. It also confirms the President's appointments to the Cabinet, the federal courts, and other high offices.

Congress has the power to impeach federal officials, including the President, Vice President, and Justices of the Supreme Court, for treason, bribery, or other high crimes and misdemeanors. The House of Representatives has the sole power to impeach, and the Senate conducts the trial. A two-thirds vote of Senators present is required for conviction.

The penalties for conviction include removal from office and, by separate Senate vote, possible disqualification from holding future federal office.

THE DEPARTMENTS OF THE U. S. GOVERNMENT

Each department of the United States Government is headed by a member of the President's Cabinet, appointed by the President and confirmed by the Senate.

The Department of State, headed by the Secretary of State, is responsible for the foreign affairs of the United States. It manages diplomatic relations with other nations, negotiates treaties (subject to Senate approval), issues passports, and maintains the Great Seal of the United States and official state records.

The Department of the Treasury, under the Secretary of the Treasury, administers the financial affairs of the United States Government. Its duties include managing federal revenue, collecting taxes, issuing currency and coins, managing government debt, and overseeing the nation's financial systems.

The Department of War, under the Secretary of War, has charge of all affairs of the United States armed forces. This includes military personnel, training, equipment, land, sea, air, and space operations, national defense strategy, and the conduct of warfare across all domains.

The Department of Justice, headed by the Attorney General, enforces the laws of the United States and represents the federal government in legal matters. It oversees federal law enforcement agencies, prosecutes violations of federal law, and provides legal advice to the President and executive departments.

The Department of the Interior, under the Secretary of the Interior, manages the nation's public lands and natural resources. It oversees national parks, wildlife refuges, energy and mineral resources on federal lands, Native American affairs, and certain responsibilities relating to U.S. territories.

The Department of Agriculture is responsible for developing and executing federal policies related to farming, agriculture, forestry, and food. It supports farmers and ranchers, conducts agricultural research, promotes conservation of natural resources, and administers food assistance and nutrition programs.

The Department of Commerce promotes economic growth, trade, and technological advancement. It oversees the Census Bureau, supports industry and trade, manages standards and measurements, provides weather forecasting, and promotes innovation and economic development.

The Department of Labor promotes the welfare of workers by improving working conditions, protecting wages and benefits, expanding employment opportunities, and enforcing labor laws. It collects labor statistics, administers workplace safety regulations, oversees unemployment programs, and enforces laws related to fair labor standards.

The Department of Health and Human Services oversees public health, medical care, and social services. It administers programs like Medicare and Medicaid, regulates food and drug safety, supports biomedical research, and addresses health crises and disease prevention.

The Department of Housing and Urban Development manages programs related to housing needs, urban development, and community revitalization. It provides affordable housing assistance, enforces fair housing laws, and supports community development initiatives.

The Department of Transportation develops and enforces policies for efficient and safe transportation systems. It oversees highways, railroads, aviation, maritime transport, public transit, and pipeline safety.

The Department of Energy advances energy security,

scientific innovation, and environmental cleanup. It manages nuclear weapons programs, promotes energy research and efficiency, oversees national laboratories, and handles energy policy.

The Department of Education promotes student achievement and ensures equal access to education. It administers federal funding for education, enforces civil rights in schools, collects education data, and supports programs for students and institutions.

The Department of Veterans Affairs provides healthcare, benefits, and services to veterans and their families. It administers medical care, disability compensation, education benefits, and memorial services for those who served.

The Department of Homeland Security protects the United States from threats including terrorism, natural disasters, cyberattacks, and border security issues. It coordinates immigration enforcement, emergency response, cybersecurity, transportation security, and intelligence analysis.

The Monroe Doctrine

What we know as the Monroe Doctrine is not a law of the United States but a part of President James Monroe's annual message to Congress on December 2, 1823. Several South American countries had recently declared their independence of Spain, and a combination of European powers was planning to send an army to subdue the new republics. Whereupon President Monroe, in his message to Congress, stated that the United States would regard as an unfriendly act any effort of a European government to extend its influence in the Western Hemisphere, or to control in any way the political destiny of any country whose independence had been recognized by this country. Although Congress took no action, this policy was generally accepted by European powers at the time and has thus been accepted ever since. It has been invoked by successive American Presidents, and generally accepted as a principle of the United States foreign policy.

President Monroe's Message

Following is the excerpt from President Monroe's message of 1823, which we think of as the Monroe Doctrine: "We owe it, therefore, to candor and to the amicable relations existing between the United States and those powers (the

European nations planning to invade South America) to declare that we should consider any attempt on their part to extend their system to any portion of the hemisphere as dangerous to our peace and safety. With the existing colonies or dependencies of any European power we have not interfered and shall not interfere. But with the governments who have declared their independence and maintained it, and whose independence we have on great consideration and on just principles, acknowledged, we could not view any interposition for the purpose of oppressing them or controlling in any other manner their destiny by any European power in any other light than as the manifestation of an unfriendly disposition toward the United States."

Part Three

THE AMERICAN VOICE

How Americans speak about freedom

Immortal American Speeches

I AM AN AMERICAN. I am inspired by the words that have guided our nation.

America's progress is often revealed through the words spoken by its leaders. These selected speeches have shaped our nation and continue to speak to the present moment.

THE CALL TO ARMS
Patrick Henry 1775

Patrick Henry has been called "the tongue of the Revolution," and this speech brought about more far-reaching results than perhaps any one speech in our history. Irritated by the timidity of certain conservative members in the Revolutionary Convention, meeting in St. John's Church in Richmond, Mr. Henry jumped to his feet and delivered his fiery oration extemporaneously.

By the time he was through, the delegates were trembling with excitement and began to shout: "To arms! To arms!" The speech resulted in more vigorous resistance to King George III, not only in Virginia but throughout the colonies.

Mr. President, it is natural to man to indulge in the illusions of hope. We are apt to shut our eyes against a painful truth. Is this the part of wise men, engaged in a great and arduous struggle for liberty? Are we disposed to be of the number of those, who, having eyes, see not, and having ears, hear not, the things which so nearly concern their temporal salvation? For my part, whatever anguish of spirit it may cost, I am willing to know the whole truth; to know the worst, and to provide for it.

I have but one lamp by which my feet are guided; and that is the lamp of experience. I know of no way of judging of the future but by the past. Let us not, I beseech you, sir, deceive ourselves longer. Sir, we have done everything that could be done to avert the storm which is now coming on. We have petitioned; we have remonstrated; we have supplicated; we ve have prostrated ourselves before the throne, and have implored its interposition to arrest the tyrannical hands of the ministry and Parliament. Our petitions have been slighted; our remonstrances have produced additional violence and insult; our supplications have been disregarded; and we have been spurned, with contempt, from the foot of the throne! In vain, after these things, may we indulge the fond hope of peace and reconciliation. There is no longer any room for hope. If we wish to be free–if we mean to preserve inviolate those inestimable privileges for which we have been so long contending–if we mean not basely to abandon the noble struggle in which we have been so long engaged, and which we have pledged ourselves never to abandon, until the glorious object of our contest shall be obtained–we must fight! I repeat it, sir, we must fight! An appeal to arms and to the God of Hosts is all that is left us!

They tell us, sir, that we are weak-unable to cope with so formidable an adversary. But when shall we be stronger? Will it be the next week, or the next year? Will it be when we are totally disarmed? Shall we acquire the means of effectual resistance by lying supinely on our backs and hugging the delusive phantom of hope, until our enemies shall have bound us hand and foot?

Sir, we are not weak if we make a a proper use of those means which the God of nature has placed in our power. Three millions of people armed in the holy cause of liberty, and in such a country as that which we possess, are invincible by any force which our enemy can send against us. Besides, sir, we shall not fight our battles alone. There is a just God who presides over the destinies of nations, and who will raise up friends to fight our battles for us. The battle, sir, is not to the strong alone; it is to the vigilant, the active, the brave.

It is in vain, sir, to extenuate the matter. Gentlemen may cry *"Peace, peace"*–but there is no peace. The war is actually begun! Our brethren are already in the field!

Why stand we here idle? What is it that gentlemen wish? What would they have? Is life so dear, or peace so sweet, as to be purchased at the price of chains and slavery? Forbid it, Almighty God! I know not what course others may take; but as for me, give me liberty or give me death!

Constitutional Convention Address on Prayer
Benjamin Franklin 1787

In the summer of 1787, delegates from thirteen states gathered in Philadelphia to draft a Constitution for a new nation. As debates grew long and tensions ran high, the framers faced not only political challenges but the human limits of patience, judgment, and unity. On June 28, Benjamin Franklin rose to remind his colleagues of a guiding principle that had shaped the American experiment from its earliest days: reliance on divine providence.

Franklin urged the delegates to seek wisdom through prayer, not as a matter of ceremony, but as a recognition that human reason alone was not enough to secure justice, liberty, and the success of the Republic. His words carried humility, gravity, and a call to unity, reflecting a sentiment deeply woven into the founding of the United States: that the nation's strength depends on both human effort and higher guidance. Though brief and often overlooked, Franklin's appeal reminds Americans that even the architects of the Constitution acknowledged forces greater than themselves in the shaping of a free nation.

> Mr. President: The small progress we have made after 4 or five weeks close attendance & continual reasonings with each other–our different sentiments on almost every question, several of the last producing as many noes as ays, is methinks a melancholy proof of the imperfection of the Human Understanding. We indeed seem to feel our own want of political wisdom, since we have been running about in search of it. We have gone back to ancient history for models of government, and examined the different forms of

those Republics which having been formed with the seeds of their own dissolution now no longer exist. And we have viewed Modern States all round Europe, but find none of their Constitutions suitable to our circumstances.

In this situation of this Assembly groping as it were in the dark to find political truth, and scarce able to distinguish it when presented to us, how has it happened, Sir, that we have not hitherto once thought of humbly applying to the Father of lights to illuminate our understandings? In the beginning of the contest with G. Britain, when we were sensible of danger we had daily prayer in this room for the Divine Protection. –Our prayers, Sir, were heard, and they were graciously answered. All of us who were engaged in the struggle must have observed frequent instances of a Superintending providence in our favor. To that kind providence we owe this happy opportunity of consulting in peace on the means of establishing our future national felicity. And have we now forgotten that powerful friend? Or do we imagine that we no longer need His assistance.

I have lived, Sir, a long time and the longer I live, the more convincing proofs I see of this truth–that God governs in the affairs of men. And if a sparrow cannot fall to the ground without His notice, is it probable that an empire can rise without His aid? We have been assured, Sir, in the sacred writings that "except the Lord build the House they labor in vain that build it." I firmly believe this; and I also believe that without His concurring aid we shall succeed in this political building no better than the Builders of Babel: We shall be divided by our little partial local interests; our projects will be confounded, and we ourselves shall be become a reproach and a bye word down to future age. And what is worse, mankind may hereafter from this unfortunate instance, despair of establishing Governments by Human Wisdom, and leave it to chance, war, and conquest.

I therefore beg leave to move–that henceforth prayers imploring the assistance of Heaven, and its blessings on our deliberations, be held in this Assembly every morning before we proceed to business, and that one or more of the Clergy of this City be requested to officiate in that service.

AVOID FOREIGN ENTANGLEMENTS
George Washington 1797

As George Washington prepared to leave the presidency, the United States was still a young and fragile nation, surrounded by powerful empires and uncertain alliances. With hard-earned experience and a long view of history, Washington warned that permanent foreign alliances could endanger American independence, drag the nation into unnecessary conflicts, and distract it from strengthening its own unity and institutions.

Though written more than two centuries ago, Washington's caution remains strikingly relevant. In an age of global conflicts, shifting alliances, and international pressures, his counsel challenges each generation of Americans to weigh involvement abroad carefully—guarding national sovereignty while acting with wisdom, restraint, and a clear sense of national interest.

Against the insidious wiles of foreign influence (I conjure you to believe me, fellow citizens) the jealousy of a free people ought to be constantly awake; since history and experience prove that foreign influence is one of the most baneful foes of Republican government. But that jealousy, to be useful, must be impartial; else it becomes the instrument of the very influence to be avoided, instead of a defense against it. Excessive partiality for one foreign nation, and excessive dislike of another, cause those whom they actuate to see danger only on one side and serve to veil and even second the arts of influence on the other.

It is our true policy to steer clear of permanent alliances with any portion of the foreign world; so far, I mean, as we are now at liberty to do it.

Harmony, liberal intercourse with all nations, are recommended by policy, humanity, and interest. But even our commercial policy should hold an equal and impartial hand; neither seeking nor granting exclusive favors or preferences; consulting the natural course of things. Constantly keeping in view that it is folly in one nation to look for disinterested favors from another; that it must pay with a portion of its independence for whatever it may accept under that character. There can be no greater error than to expect or calculate upon real favors from nation to nation. It is an illusion, which experience must cure, which a just pride ought to discard.

THE PEOPLE'S GOVERNMENT
Daniel Webster 1830

Daniel Webster has been called America's greatest orator, and his *"Reply to Hayne"* is considered his masterpiece. In a speech to the Senate Robert Y. Hayne of South Carolina had come out openly in favor of the doctrine of nullification, or the right of a state to set aside any act of the United States, if it considered such an act unconstitutional.

Senator Webster, whose first consideration always was to strengthen the Union, had only one night to prepare a reply. His speech, which created a profound impression at the time and is now a part of our political belief, stated clearly the differences which thirty years later were to divide North and South in the War Between the States.

> This leads us to inquire into the origin of this government and the source of its power. Whose agent is it? Is it the creature of the state legislators, or the creature of the people? If the government of the United States be the agent of the State governments, then they may control it, provided they can agree in the manner of controlling it; if it be the agent of the people, then the people alone can control it, restrain it, modify, or reform it. It is observable enough that the doctrine for which the honorable gentleman, Mr. Hayne, contends leads him to the necessity of maintaining, not only that this general government is the creature of the States, but that it is the creature of each of the States severally, so that each may assert the power for itself of determining whether it acts within the limits of its authority.

> It is the servant of four and twenty masters, of different

wills and different purposes, and yet bound to obey all. This absurdity (for it seems no less) arises from a misconception as to the origin of this government and its true character. It is, sir, the people's Constitution, the people's government, made for the people, made by the people, and answerable to the people. The people of the United States have declared that this Constitution shall be the supreme law. We must either admit the proposition or dispute their authority.

We are here to administer a Constitution emanating immediately from the people, and trusted by them to our administration. It is not the creature of the State governments.

I profess, sir, in my career hitherto to have kept steadily in view the prosperity and honor of the whole country and the preservation of our federal Union. It is to that Union we owe our safety at home and our consideration and dignity abroad. It is to that Union that we are chiefly indebted for whatever makes us most proud of our country. That Union we reached only by the discipline of our virtues in the severe school of adversity. It had its origin in the necessities of disordered finance, prostrate commerce, and ruined credit. Under its benign influence those great interests im- mediately awoke, as from the dead, and sprang forth with newness of life. Every year of its duration has teemed with fresh proofs of its utility and its blessings; and although our territory has stretched out wider and wider and our population spread farther and farther, they have not outrun its protection or its benefits. It has been to us all a copious fountain of national, social, and personal happiness.

While the Union lasts we have high, exciting, gratifying prospects spread out before us for us and our children. Beyond that I seek not to penetrate the veil. God grant that in my day at least that curtain may not rise! God grant that on on my vision never may be opened what lies behind! When my eyes shall be turned to behold for the last time the sun in heaven, may I not see him shining on the broken and dishonored fragments of a once glorious Union; on States dissevered, discordant, belligerent; on a land rent with civil feuds, or drenched, it may be, in fraternal blood! Let their last feeble and lingering glance rather behold the gorgeous ensign of the Republic, now known and honored throughout the earth, still full high advanced, its arms and trophies streaming in their original lustre, not a stripe erased or polluted, nor a single star obscured, bearing for its motto no such miserable interrogatory as, *"What is all this worth?"* nor those other words of delusion and folly, *"Liberty first and Union afterward"*; but everywhere, spread all over in characters of living light, blazing on all its ample folds, as they float over the sea and over the land, and in every wind under the whole heavens, that other sentiment dear to every American heart–Liberty and Union, now and forever, one and inseparable!

THE GETTYSBURG ADDRESS
Abraham Lincoln 1863

Today the Gettysburg Address is considered the greatest gem of oratory the world has produced, but at the time Abraham Lincoln thought the speech was a failure. He had written it hastily on the back of an envelope while en route by train to Gettysburg, to be present at the dedication of the Gettysburg battlefield. The orator of the day was Edward Everett whose polished address held the attention of the crowd for two hours. Then Abraham Lincoln arose–a tall, awkward figure–and said only a few words. But those few words, some of the most beautiful in the English language, have come ringing down the years, to inspire every true American and all others who love freedom.

Four score and seven years ago our fathers brought forth upon this continent, a new nation, conceived in Liberty, and dedicated to the proposition that all men are created equal.

Now we are engaged in a great civil war, testing whether that nation, or any nation so conceived, and so dedicated, can long endure. We are met on a great battlefield of that war. We have come to dedicate a portion of that field, as a final resting place for those who here gave their lives, that that nation might live.

It is altogether fitting and proper that we should do this. But, in a larger sense, we cannot dedicate–we cannot consecrate–we cannot hallow–this ground.

The brave men, living and dead, who struggled here, have consecrated it, far above our poor power to add or detract. The world will little note, nor long remember, what we say here, but it can never forget what they did here.

It is for us, the living, rather, to be dedicated here to the unfinished work which they who fought here, have, thus far, so nobly advanced.

It is rather for us to be here dedicated to the great task remaining before us–that from these honored dead we take increased devotion to that cause for which they here gave the last full measure of devotion-that we here highly resolve that these dead shall not have died in vain-that this nation, under God, shall have a new birth of freedom–and that, government of the people, by the people, for the people, shall not perish from the earth.

AMERICA FOR ALL
Theodore Roosevelt 1912

This speech was delivered on the eve of the Republican Convention in 1912. Although it failed to bring Theodore Roosevelt the Republican nomination for the Presidency, his enthusiastic supporters bolted the party and nominated him as the candidate of a third (the Progressive) party.

Believing that William Howard Taft, in his term as President, had failed to carry out certain progressive policies, Theodore Roosevelt called this address the Armageddon Speech. This was a name used in the Book of Revelation (ch. xvi) for the last great battle between the forces of good and evil. The words express an American–democratic conviction.

A period of change is upon us. Our opponents, the men of inaction, ask us to stand still. But we could not stand still if we would. We must either go forward or go backward. Never was the need more imperative than now for men of vision who are also men of action.

We who stand for the cause of progress are fighting to make this country a better place to live in for those who have been harshly treated by fate; and, if we succeed, it will also be a better place for those who are well off.

We stand for the cause of the uplift of humanity and the betterment of mankind. We are pledged to eternal war against wrong, whether by the few or the many, by a plutocracy or by a mob. We believe that this country will not be a permanently good place for any of us to live in, unless we make it a reasonably good place for all of us to live in.

The sons of all of us will pay in the future, if we of the present do not do justice to all in the present. Our cause is the cause of justice for all in the interest of all. The present contest is but a phase of the larger struggle. Assuredly the fight will go on, whether we win or lose; but it will be a sore disaster to lose. What happens to me is not of the slightest consequence. I am to be used, as in a doubtful battle any man is used, to his hurt or not, so long as he is useful, and is then cast aside or left to die.

I wish you to feel this. I mean it; and I shall need no sympathy when you are through with me; for this fight is far too great to permit us to concern ourselves about any one man's welfare. If we are true to ourselves by putting far above our own interests the triumph of the high cause for which we battle, we shall not lose.

We fight in honorable fashion for the good of mankind; fearless of the future, unheeding of our individual fates, with unflinching hearts and undimmed eyes; we stand at Armageddon, and we battle for the Lord.

THE RIGHTS OF MANKIND
Woodrow Wilson 1917

Not since the time of Abraham Lincoln had there been a speech which so stirred the people of his own country, and of the world, as Woodrow Wilson's address recommending to Congress that the United States take up arms against Germany in the first World War.

As a man who profoundly loved peace, the President had hoped almost up until the last that our country would be able to avoid war. His hands were seen to tremble as he stood up before both houses of Congress to read his Message, which is considered one of the great state papers of all time. By the time he had finished, many of his listeners were in tears; then cheer after cheer rang through the halls of Congress. The Message was read throughout the world, bringing new hope to millions of oppressed peoples.

> While we do these things, these deeply momentous things, let us be very clear, and make very clear to all the world what our motives and our objects are.

We are glad, now that we see the facts with no veil of false pretense about them, to fight thus for the ultimate peace of the world and for the liberation of its peoples–the German people included–for the rights of nations great and small and the privilege of men everywhere to choose their way of life and of obedience. The world must be made safe for democracy. Its peace must be planted upon the trusted foundations of political liberty. We have no selfish ends to serve. We desire no conquest, no dominion. We seek no indemnities for ourselves, no material compensation for the sacrifices we shall freely make. We are but one of the champions of the rights of mankind. We shall be satisfied when those rights have been made as secure as the faith and the freedom of the nation can make them.

It is a distressing and oppressive duty, Gentlemen of the Congress, which I have performed in thus addressing you. There are, it may be, many months of fiery trial and sacrifice ahead of us. It is a fearful thing to lead this great peaceful people into war, into the most terrible and disastrous of all wars, civilization itself seeming to be in the balance. But the right is more precious than peace, and we shall fight for the things which we have always carried nearest our hearts, for democracy, for the right of those who submit to authority to to have a voice in their own governments, for the rights and liberties of small nations, for a universal dominion of right by such a concert of free peoples as shall bring peace and safety to all nations and make the world itself at last free.

To such a task we can dedicate our lives and our fortunes, everything that we are and everything that we have, with the pride of those who know that the day has come when America is privileged to spend her blood and her might for the principles that gave her birth and happiness and the peace which she has treasured. God helping her, she can do no other.

PEARL HARBOR ADDRESS TO THE NATION
Franklin D. Roosevelt 1941

On December 8, 1941—less than 24 hours after the surprise attack on Pearl Harbor—the United States stood stunned, angry, and suddenly united. The American people awoke to the reality that the nation was no longer watching a distant war from across the oceans; it had been violently drawn into it. Shock quickly hardened into resolve as citizens looked to their president for clarity, reassurance, and direction in a moment of national crisis.

President Franklin D. Roosevelt delivered his address to a joint session of Congress just after noon, speaking for only about seven minutes, yet shaping the course of American history. Carefully composed the night before with the help of close advisors, Roosevelt deliberately revised the opening line to describe December 7 as "a date which will live in infamy," capturing the nation's sense of betrayal and moral outrage. Although confined to a wheelchair, Roosevelt projected calm authority and moral certainty, framing the attack not only as an assault on American territory but on the principles of peace and international order.

Broadcast live by radio across the country, the speech reached millions of Americans gathered around their sets in homes, shops, and factories. Its direct language and measured tone reflected both the grief and determination of the people it addressed. Within an hour of the speech's conclusion, Congress overwhelmingly approved a declaration of war against Japan, marking the moment when national shock gave way to unified purpose and the United States formally entered World War II.

Mr. Vice President, and Mr. Speaker, and Members of the Senate and House of Representatives:

Yesterday, December 7, 1941—a date which will live in infamy—the United States of America was suddenly and deliberately attacked by naval and air forces of the

Empire of Japan.

The United States was at peace with that Nation and, at the solicitation of Japan, was still in conversation with its Government and its Emperor looking toward the maintenance of peace in the Pacific. Indeed, one hour after Japanese air squadrons had commenced bombing in the American Island of Oahu, the Japanese Ambassador to the United States and his colleague delivered to our Secretary of State a formal reply to a recent American message. And while this reply stated that it seemed useless to continue the existing diplomatic negotiations, it contained no threat or hint of war or of armed attack.

It will be recorded that the distance of Hawaii from Japan makes it obvious that the attack was deliberately planned many days or even weeks ago. During the intervening time the Japanese Government has deliberately sought to deceive the United States by false statements and expressions of hope for continued peace.

The attack yesterday on the Hawaiian Islands has caused severe damage to American naval and military forces. I regret to tell you that very many American lives have been lost. In addition American ships have been reported torpedoed on the high seas between San Francisco and Honolulu.

Yesterday the Japanese Government also launched an attack against Malaya. Last night Japanese forces attacked Hong Kong. Last night Japanese forces attacked Guam. Last night Japanese forces attacked the Philippine Islands. Last night the Japanese attacked

Wake Island. And this morning the Japanese attacked Midway Island.

Japan has, therefore, undertaken a surprise offensive extending throughout the Pacific area. The facts of yesterday and today speak for themselves. The people of the United States have already formed their opinions and well understand the implications to the very life and safety of our Nation.

As Commander in Chief of the Army and Navy I have directed that all measures be taken for our defense.

But always will our whole Nation remember the character of the onslaught against us.

No matter how long it may take us to overcome this premeditated invasion, the American people in their righteous might will win through to absolute victory. I believe that I interpret the will of the Congress and of the people when I assert that we will not only defend ourselves to the uttermost but will make it very certain that this form of treachery shall never again endanger us.

Hostilities exist. There is no blinking at the fact that our people, our territory, and our interests are in grave danger.

With confidence in our armed forces—with the unbounding determination of our people—we will gain the inevitable triumph- so help us God.

I ask that the Congress declare that since the unprovoked and dastardly attack by Japan on Sunday,

December 7, 1941, a state of war has existed between the United States and the Japanese Empire.

BRANDENBURG GATE SPEECH
Ronald Reagan 1987

On June 12, 1987, President Ronald Reagan stood before the Brandenburg Gate in West Berlin, facing one of the most powerful symbols of division in modern history—the Berlin Wall. For more than 25 years, the wall had separated families, silenced freedom, and stood as a concrete reminder of the Cold War struggle between liberty and authoritarian control. Though tensions between the United States and the Soviet Union were easing, many believed the wall was permanent. Reagan did not.

Speaking directly to both the free world and the leaders of the Soviet Union, Reagan framed the conflict not merely as a political dispute, but as a moral one. His words echoed a core American belief: that freedom is not granted by governments, but is the natural right of all people. The now-famous challenge—"Mr. Gorbachev, tear down this wall!"—was bold, controversial, and dismissed by some as unrealistic. Yet it captured the spirit of a nation that believed history bends toward liberty when courage speaks plainly.

Less than three years later, the Berlin Wall fell. Reagan's speech endures not because it predicted the moment, but because it affirmed an American conviction repeated throughout history: freedom must be spoken, defended, and passed on. As Reagan himself warned, it is always *"only one generation away from extinction."*

We come to Berlin, we American Presidents, because it's our duty to speak, in this place, of freedom. But I must confess, we're drawn here by other things as well: by the feeling of history in this city; by the air of excitement and hope; by the promise of tomorrow.

Standing before the Brandenburg Gate, every man is a German separated from his fellow men. Every man is a Berliner, forced to look upon a scar.

President von Weizsäcker has said, *"The German question is open as long as the Brandenburg Gate is closed."* Today I say: As long as this gate is closed, as long as this scar of a wall is permitted to stand, it is not the German question alone that remains open, but the question of freedom for all mankind.

Yet I do not come here to lament. For I find in Berlin a message of hope, even in the shadow of this wall, a message of triumph.

In this season of spring in Berlin, the city is bursting with life. In the Tiergarten, people are sunning themselves. Flowers are blooming everywhere. In Berlin, humor is everywhere. In Berlin, as in all Germany, people are adapting, reinventing themselves. In Berlin, a wall cannot stop spring.

The wall cannot suppress hope. The wall cannot crush faith. The wall cannot destroy truth.

The wall cannot survive freedom.

As you look out over the Brandenburg Gate, the symbol of German unity, remember that while the wall divides, it also invites us to think of the future.

General Secretary Gorbachev, if you seek peace, if you seek prosperity for the Soviet Union and Eastern Europe, if you seek liberalization: Come here to this gate!

Mr. Gorbachev, open this gate!

Mr. Gorbachev, tear down this wall!

I understand the fear of war and the pain of division that afflict this continent—and I pledge to you my country's efforts to help overcome these burdens. To be sure, we must stand together in the struggle to reduce arms. We must work to make peace real.

And yet we cannot forget that the wall was put up to stop those whose faith and ideals would not withstand free choice. The wall was erected not to keep people in—but to keep people out.

Today, freedom leads to prosperity. Freedom replaces the ancient hatreds among the nations with comity and peace. Freedom is the victor.

In the West, we believe in the dignity of man. In the East, they believe in the power of the state. In the West, freedom is indivisible; in the East, it is dispensed by the state.

Today, the world stands at a crossroads. We must choose freedom.

This wall will fall. Beliefs become reality. Yes, across Europe, this wall will fall. For it cannot withstand faith;

it cannot withstand truth; it cannot withstand freedom.

And I say to you tonight: Let us make sure that history says of us that we did all that could be done. Let us resolve that the walls which divide us—whether physical, economic, or ideological—will be torn down.

Freedom is the right of all God's children.

Thank you, and God bless you all.

ADDRESS TO A JOINT SESSION OF CONGRESS
George W. Bush 2001

On September 20, 2001, nine days after the terrorist attacks of September 11, President George W. Bush addressed a joint session of Congress and a nation still reeling from shock and grief. Nearly 3,000 lives had been lost, American soil had been attacked, and citizens were searching for meaning, resolve, and reassurance. The country was united in mourning—and bracing for what would come next.

Bush's address sought to steady the nation and define the moment. He made clear that the attacks were not only acts of terror, but a direct assault on freedom itself. Framing the conflict as a moral struggle between civilization and barbarism, he called Americans—and the world—to resolve, vigilance, and unity. The speech marked a turning point, as the United States committed itself to confronting global terrorism and reaffirmed a long-held American conviction: that freedom must be defended, even at great cost.

Mr. Speaker, Mr. President Pro Tempore, Members

of Congress, and fellow Americans:

In the normal course of events, Presidents come to this chamber to report on the state of the Union. Tonight, no such report is needed. It has already been delivered by the American people.

We have seen the state of our Union in the courage of rescuers, working past exhaustion. We have seen the state of our Union in the determination of parents who have lost their children, yet refused to give in to despair. We have seen the state of our Union in the sturdy souls of rescuers digging through rubble and in the willingness of Americans to give blood and money and help in any way they could.

The attacks on September the 11th made America a battlefield—but the freedom-loving world did not change. Our responsibility to history did not change. Our duties to ourselves and to our children did not change.

The terrorists' directive commands them to kill Christians and Jews, to kill all Americans, and make no distinction among military and civilians, including women and children. This is not a conflict between civilizations. It is a conflict between civilization and barbarism.

Americans are asking: Who attacked our country? The evidence we have gathered all points to a collection of loosely affiliated terrorist organizations known as al Qaeda. They are the same murderers indicted for bombing American embassies in Tanzania and Kenya, and responsible for bombing the USS Cole.

The leadership of al Qaeda has great influence in Afghanistan and supports the Taliban regime in controlling most of that country. The Taliban must act, and act immediately.

They will hand over the terrorists, or they will share in their fate.

I also want to speak tonight directly to Muslims throughout the world. We respect your faith. It's practiced freely by many millions of Americans, and by millions more in countries that America counts as friends. Its teachings are good and peaceful, and those who commit evil in the name of Allah blaspheme the name of Allah.

Tonight, I ask for your patience, with the understanding that America acts not in anger, but in resolve.

Our war on terror begins with al Qaeda, but it does not end there. It will not end until every terrorist group of global reach has been found, stopped, and defeated.

Americans are asking: Why do they hate us? They hate what we see right here in this chamber—a democratically elected government. Their leaders are self-appointed. They hate our freedoms—our freedom of religion, our freedom of speech, our freedom to vote and assemble and disagree with each other.

These terrorists kill not merely to end lives, but to disrupt and end a way of life. This is the fight of all who believe in progress and pluralism, tolerance and freedom.

Every nation, in every region, now has a decision to make. Either you are with us, or you are with the terrorists. From this day forward, any nation that continues to harbor or support terrorism will be regarded by the United States as a hostile regime.

Our nation is patient and resolute. We will not tire, we will not falter, and we will not fail.

The course of this conflict is not known, yet its outcome is certain. Freedom and fear, justice and cruelty, have always been at war, and we know that God is not neutral between them.

We will direct every resource at our command—every means of diplomacy, every tool of intelligence, every instrument of law enforcement, every financial influence, and every necessary weapon of war—to the disruption and to the defeat of the global terror network.

This is the world's fight. This is civilization's fight. This is the fight of all who believe in the progress and pluralism, tolerance and freedom.

And we ask every nation to join us.

We will not forget this wound to our country, nor those who inflicted it. We will not yield to fear. We will not forget our responsibility to defend freedom.

Great harm has been done to us. We have suffered great loss. And in our grief and anger, we have found our mission and our moment.

Freedom and fear are at war. The advance of human

freedom—the great achievement of our time and the great hope of every time—now depends on us.

Tonight, we are a country awakened to danger and called to defend freedom. Our grief has turned to anger, and anger to resolution.

Whether we bring our enemies to justice, or bring justice to our enemies, justice will be done.

God bless America.

Watchwords of Democracy

I AM AN AMERICAN. I am proud of these watchwords of democracy.

Certain ringing phrases, spoken in time of crisis, have become a part of the American way of thinking. These phrases have become our watchwords. We repeat them and are inspired by them, often forgetting, sometimes without even knowing, the names of the men who first said them or the circumstances which called them forth.

"Let us raise a standard to which the wise and honest can repair; the rest is in the hands of God."

> – George Washington in a speech to the Constitutional Convention (1787).

"We must all hang together, or assuredly we shall all hang separately."

> – Remark by Benjamin Franklin after the signing of the Declaration of Independence (1776).

"To be prepared for war is one of the most effectual means of preserving peace."

> -George Washington in his first annual address to both houses of Congress (1790).

"Is life so dear, or peace so sweet, as to be purchased at the price of chains and slavery? Forbid it, Almighty God! I know not what course others may take, but as for me, give me liberty or give me ne death!"

– Patrick Henry in a speech before the Virginia Convention in St. John's Episcopal Church, Richmond, Virginia (1775).

"To the memory of the Man, first in war, first in peace, and first in the hearts of his countrymen."

– Colonel Henry Lee in a eulogy delivered after the death of Washington (1799).

"The God who gave us life gave us liberty at the same time."

– Thomas Jefferson in "Summary View of the Rights of British America" (1774).

"I would rather be exposed to the inconveniences attending too much liberty than to those attending too small a degree of it."

-Thomas Jefferson in a letter (1791).

"I have not yet begun to fight."

– John Paul Jones, when called upon to surrender in a battle at sea. Though his ship, the Bon Homme Richard, was sinking under him he refused to give up, and the battle ended by his capturing the British ship, the Serapis, and sailing it, with his crew, in safety to France (1779).

"These are times that try men's souls."

– Thomas Paine, in an article-"The American Crisis"-in the Pennsylvania Magazine (1776).

"Equal and exact justice to all men, freedom of religion, freedom of the press, freedom of person under the protection of the habeas corpus; and trial by juries impartially selected these principles form the bright constellation which has gone before us."

– Thomas Jefferson in his first inaugural (1801).

"I only regret that I have but one life to lose for my country."

– Nathan Hale, in a speech he made just before being hanged by the enemy as a spy (1776).

"Men, you are all marksmen–don't one of you fire until you see the whites of their eyes."

–Israel Putnam at Battle of Bunker Hill (1775); also attributed to Colonel William Prescott.

"Millions for defense but not one cent for tribute."

– Attributed to Charles Cotesworth Pinckney, when ambassador to the French Republic. He referred to a recent demand from France for a loan, which was really a bribe for refraining from plundering American merchant vessels (1797).

"Liberty and union, now and forever, one and inseparable!"

– Daniel Webster, in a public address (1830).

"Our Federal Union: it must be preserved."

– Andrew Jackson in a toast given at the Jefferson Birthday Celebration (1830).

"Don't give up the ship! You will beat them off!"

– The dying words of Captain James Mugford of the schooner, Franklin, during a British attack in Boston Harbor (1776). The words, "Don't give up the ship," have also been attributed to a number of other commanders.

"I shall know but one country...I was born an American; I live an American; I shall die an American."

– Daniel Webster, in a speech (1850).

"Now he belongs to the ages."

– Edwin M. Stanton, Secretary of War, at the deathbed of Lincoln (1865).

"I would rather be right than President."

– Henry Clay's answer when told that he was injuring his chances of becoming President because he was advocating certain compromise measures (1850).

"Driven from every other corner of the earth, Freedom of Thought and The Right of Private Judgment in matters of conscience direct their course to this happy country as their last asylum."

– Samuel Adams, in a speech (1776).

"We have met the enemy and they are ours–two ships, two brigs, one schooner and one sloop."

– Commodore Oliver Hazard Perry, to General William Henry Harrison, in announcing a victory over the English in the Battle of Lake Erie (1813).

"That nation has not lived in vain which has given the world Washington and Lincoln, the best great men and the greatest good men whom history can show"

– Henry Cabot Lodge, in a "Lincoln" address before the Massachusetts legislature (1909).

"I have not permitted myself, gentlemen, to conclude that I am the best man in the country, but I am reminded in this connection of an old Dutch farmer who remarked that it was not best to swap horses while crossing stream"

> – Abraham Lincoln, in a speech.

"At what point then is the approach of danger to be expected? I answer if it ever reach us it must spring up amongst us; it cannot come from abroad. If destruction be our lot, we must ourselves be its author and finisher. As a nation of free men, we must live through all time or die by suicide."

> – Abraham Lincoln, in an address on the "Perpetuation of our Political Institution."

"The government, with its institutions, belongs to the people who inhabit it. Whenever they shall grow weary of the existing government, they can exercise their constitutional right of amending it, or their revolutionary right to dismember or overthrow it."

> – Abraham Lincoln, in a speech before the first Republican state convention in Illinois (1856).

"God reigns and the Government at Washington lives."

> – James A. Garfield, in a speech delivered in New York City, to a crowd distressed by news of Lincoln's assassination (1865).

"Public office is a public trust."

> – William C. Hudson, a newspaper man, produced this slogan from the various speeches of Grover Cleveland during his first campaign for the Presidency (1884).

"Remember the Maine!"

> – Slogan of the Spanish-American War, after the American battleship Maine had been destroyed in the harbor at Havana, Cuba, by a mine (1898).

"Our country! In her intercourse with foreign nations may she always be in the right; but our country, right or wrong!"

> – A toast given by Stephen Decatur at a dinner in his honor at Norfolk, Va. (1816).

"You shall not press down upon the brow of labor this crown of thorns; you shall not crucify mankind upon a cross of gold."

> – William Jennings Bryan, in a speech before the National Democratic Convention (1896).

"The humblest citizen of all the land, when clad in the armor of a righteous cause, is stronger than all the hosts of Error."

> – William Jennings Bryan in a speech at National Democratic Convention (1896).

"We have room but for one language here and that is English, for we intend to see that the crucible turns our people out as Americans, and not as dwellers in a polyglot boarding house."

> – Theodore Roosevelt, in a letter read at the All American Festival, New York (1919).

"The world must be made safe for democracy."

> – Woodrow Wilson in address to Congress, asking for a Declaration of War against Germany (1917).

"There is a homely adage which runs, 'Speak softly and carry a big stick; you will go far! If the American nation will speak softly and yet build and keep at a pitch of the highest training a thoroughly efficient navy, the Monroe Doctrine will go far."

> – Theodore Roosevelt, in a speech at Springfield, Illinois (1903).

"There are a great many hyphens left in America. For my part I think the most un-American thing in the world is a hyphen."

> – Woodrow Wilson in a speech at St. Paul (1919).

"There can be no fifty-fifty Americanism in this country. There is room here for only 100 percent Americanism, only for those who are Americans and nothing else."

> – Theodore Roosevelt, in a speech at the Republican Convention, Saratoga, N. Y.

"There is no right to strike against the public safety by anybody, anywhere, any time."

> – Calvin Coolidge, in a telegram to Samuel Gompers, President of the American Federation of Labor during the Boston police strike (1919).

"Let us have faith that right makes might; and in that faith let us to the end, dare to do our duty as we understand it."

> – Abraham Lincoln.

"The qualifications of self-government are not innate. They are the result of habit and long training, and for these they will require time and probably much suffering."

> – Thomas Jefferson.

"You can fool some of the people all of the time, and all of the people some of the time, but you cannot fool all of the people all of the time."

– Attributed to Abraham Lincoln.

"We have been taught to regard a representative of the people as a sentinel on the watch tower of liberty."

– Daniel Webster, in a speech to the Senate.

"They that can give up essential liberty to obtain a little temporary safety deserve neither liberty nor safety."

– Benjamin Franklin in "Historical Review of Pennsylvania."

"The tree of liberty must be refreshed from time to time with the blood of patriots and tyrants,"

– Thomas Jefferson on November 13, 1787, in a letter to his son-in-law's friend, William Stephens Smith.

"The only thing we have to fear is fear itself."

– Franklin D. Roosevelt, First Inaugural Address, (1933)

"Ask not what your country can do for you—ask what you can do for your country."

– John F. Kennedy, Inaugural Address, (1961)

"The most terrifying words in the English language are: I'm from the government and I'm here to help."

– Ronald Reagan, Remarks in Burbank, California, (1986)

"Injustice anywhere is a threat to justice everywhere."

– Martin Luther King Jr., Letter from Birmingham Jail, (1963)

"Government is not the solution to our problem; government is the problem."

> – Ronald Reagan, First Inaugural Address, (1981)

"I have a dream that one day this nation will rise up and live out the true meaning of its creed."

> – Martin Luther King Jr., I Have a Dream Speech, (1963)

"Government's first duty is to protect the people, not run their lives."

> – Ronald Reagan, Address to the Nation on the Economy, (1981)

"We will make no distinction between the terrorists who committed these acts and those who harbor them."

> – George W. Bush, Address to a Joint Session of Congress, (2001)

"A nation that is afraid to let its people judge the truth and falsehood in an open market is a nation that is afraid of its people."

> – John F. Kennedy, Speech on the Press, (1961)

"Freedom is never more than one generation away from extinction. It must be fought for, protected, and handed on for them to do the same."

> – Ronald Reagan, Remarks at the Phoenix, Arizona, Conservative Political Action Conference, (1961)

"I can hear you! The rest of the world hears you! And the people who knocked these buildings down will hear all of us soon!"

> — George W. Bush at Ground Zero, September 14, 2001

"If we ever forget that we are One Nation Under God, then we will be a nation gone under."

> – Ronald Reagan, Remarks at the National Prayer Breakfast, (1983)

"For years Democrats and the media kept saying that we needed new legislation to secure the border … but it turned out that all we really needed was a new President."

> – Donald J. Trump, in a 2025 speech about border security

"Within the covers of the Bible are the answers for all the problems men face."

> – Ronald Reagan, Remarks at the National Religious Broadcasters Convention, (1983)

Part Four

AMERICAN TRADITIONS AND SYMBOLS

How freedom is remembered and practiced

The Flag of the United States

I AM AN AMERICAN. I pledge my allegiance to the Flag of the United States of America.

"We take the star from Heaven, the red from our mother country, separating it by white stripes, thus showing that we have separated from her, and the white stripes shall go down to posterity representing liberty."
– George Washington

The Stars and Stripes, as we know it today, was by no means the first American flag. During the early days of the American Revolution, several flags were used. One showed a rattlesnake against a yellow background with the inscription, "Don't Tread on Me." Other flags of various designs were also flown.

On June 14, 1777, nearly a year after the Declaration of Independence, the Continental Congress adopted the following resolution:

"Resolved, That the flag of the United States be thirteen stripes, alternate red and white; that the Union be thirteen stars, white in a blue field, representing a new constellation."

It has been said that red stood for valor, white for purity, and blue for justice.

THIRTEEN STRIPES AND FIFTY STARS

The thirteen stripes and thirteen stars in the first flag represented the thirteen original states. In 1794, after two new states were admitted, Congress increased both the stripes and stars to fifteen.

By 1818, there were twenty states in the Union, and Congress enacted a law providing that the number of stripes should be restored permanently to thirteen, while a new star would be added for each new state admitted to the Union. This law remains in effect today.

Each new star becomes official on the Fourth of July following a state's admission. Today, the American flag has fifty stars, representing the fifty states, and thirteen stripes, representing the original thirteen states.

THE STORY OF BETSY ROSS

One of the most colorful stories that have grown up around the American flag is the story of Mrs. Betsy Ross. George Washington, Colonel George Ross and Robert Morris had been appointed by Congress to plan a flag, and it is told that they called on Mrs. Ross in her Arch Street home in Philadelphia to ask her to make a flag for them. It has been said that she folded a piece of paper in such a way that she was able to cut a five-pointed star with a single snip of her scissors, in order to show General Washington how a five-pointed star would look.

THE CODE OF THE FLAG

The official name of the flag is the "Flag of the United States of America."

The official description states that the flag has thirteen horizontal stripes—seven red and six white—alternating, and a union of white five-pointed stars on a blue field. The number of stars corresponds to the number of states in the Union. The current flag contains fifty stars, arranged in nine offset horizontal rows alternating between six and five stars each, each star pointing upward.

When the Flag Is Flown

The flag should be displayed on the following days, among others:

- Inauguration Day (January 20 every four years)
- Lincoln's Birthday (February 12
- Washington's Birthday / Presidents' Day (third Monday in February)
- Easter Sunday
- Mother's Day (second Sunday in May)
- Memorial Day (last Monday in May)
- Flag Day (June 14)
- Independence Day (July 4)
- Constitution Day (September 17)
- Gold Star Mother's Day (last Sunday in September)
- Columbus Day (second Monday in October)
- Veterans Day (November 11)
- Thanksgiving Day

On Memorial Day, the flag is flown at half-staff until noon, then raised to full staff for the remainder of the day.

Raising and Lowering the Flag

The flag is not raised before sunrise and is lowered sunset. In raising and lowering the flag it must not touch the ground. Those present at the ceremony should stand at attention, ready to salute.

The flag may be flown at night if properly illuminated.

Displaying the Flag

When displaying the flag on a staff, the blue field must be at the top of the staff. When the flag is displayed either vertically or horizontally against a wall, the union should be uppermost and to the flag's own right.

When the flag is displayed over a street or between two points so that both sides are visible, the union should face north on an east–west street and east on a north–south street.

Saluting the Flag

It is proper to salute the flag during the ceremony of raising or lowering it, or when it is passing in a parade or in review.

All persons present in uniform should render the military salute. Members of the Armed Forces and veterans who are present but not in uniform may render the military salute.

All other persons present should face the flag and stand at attention with their right hand over the heart. Men not in uniform, if applicable, should remove their headdress with their right hand and hold it at the left shoulder, the hand being over the heart. Women stand at attention with their right hand over the heart.

To render the military salute correctly, a person in uniform stands at attention, raises the right hand smartly to the forehead over the right eye, palm downward, fingers extended and close together, the arm at an angle of about forty-five degrees. The salute is held until the flag has passed or the ceremony concludes, then dropped smartly to the side.

When worn as a badge or lapel pin, being a replica of the flag and representing a living country considered a living thing, it should be small and properly designed. It should be pinned to the left lapel or breast near the heart. The flag must not be used as part of a costume, athletic uniform, or wearing apparel.

No advertising, lettering, designs, marks, pictures, or other additions may appear on the flag itself. Use of the flag for commercial purposes, as a trademark, or in any manner for advertising is prohibited.

Our Flag in Relation to Other Flags

The Flag of the United States has the right-hand position when carried in a parade with the flag of another country, or when crossed with the flag of another nation, and its staff should be in front of the staff of the other flag. When grouped with other flags, it takes the highest place and must be of the same height and size.

In a Public Building

When displaying a flag in the nave of a church, it should be at the congregation's right. When flown from a staff in the chancel or on a speaker's platform, the flag is at the speaker's right, slightly in front. If displayed flat on a speaker's platform, it should be above and behind the speaker, hung high enough to be above the heads of any persons sitting on the platform.

"I pledge allegiance to the Flag of the United States of America, and to the Republic for which it stands, one nation under God, indivisible, with liberty and justice for all."

The Pledge of Allegiance was written in 1892 by Francis Bellamy. When reciting the pledge, individuals stand at attention, face the flag, and place the right hand over the heart.

Songs of the Republic

I AM AN AMERICAN. I sing my country's patriotic songs.

THE STAR-SPANGLED BANNER

Our national anthem was written by Francis Scott Key, a Baltimore lawyer, after the bombardment of Fort McHenry, in 1814. He had visited the British fleet to intercede for a captured friend; and he then had been detained while the British attacked the fort. All night the battle went on, and when morning came he was overjoyed to see the Stars and Stripes still waving. Taking an old letter from his pocket, he hastily scribbled the first stanza of his poem on the back. In the boat on the way back to Baltimore, he finished it.

Soon handbills bearing the words were being distributed throughout the city. Someone suggested that the old tune, "To Anacreon," be adapted to the words, so they might be sung at once. Soon the people of Baltimore, thrilled by the recent American victory, were singing them-and then the entire nation.

Although Congress did not recognize the song officially as our national anthem until 1931, it has held first place in the hearts of Americans for many years.

O say can you see, by the dawn's early light,
What so proudly we hail'd at the twilight's last gleaming,
Whose broad stripes and bright stars through the perilous fight
O'er the ramparts we watch'd were so gallantly streaming?
And the rocket's red glare, the bomb bursting in air,
Gave proof through the night that our flag was still there,
O say does that star-spangled banner yet wave
O'er the land of the free and the home of the brave?

On the shore dimly seen through the mists of the deep
Where the foe's haughty host in dread silence reposes,
What is that which the breeze, o'er the towering steep,
As it fitfully blows, half conceals, half discloses?
Now it catches the gleam of the morning's first beam,
In full glory reflected now shines in the stream,
'Tis the star-spangled banner - O long may it wave
O'er the land of the free and the home of the brave!

And where is that band who so vauntingly swore,
That the havoc of war and the battle's confusion
A home and a Country should leave us no more?
Their blood has wash'd out their foul footstep's pollution.
No refuge could save the hireling and slave
From the terror of flight or the gloom of the grave,
And the star-spangled banner in triumph doth wave
O'er the land of the free and the home of the brave.

O thus be it ever when freemen shall stand
Between their lov'd home and the war's desolation!
Blest with vict'ry and peace may the heav'n rescued land
Praise the power that hath made and preserv'd us a nation!
Then conquer we must, when our cause it is just,
And this be our motto - "In God is our trust,"
And the star-spangled banner in triumph shall wave
O'er the land of the free and the home of the brave.

AMERICA

Our national hymn was written by Samuel Francis Smith while he was still a theological student at Andover Academy, in 1832. "I did not know at the time that the tune was the British 'God Save the King,'" he said. "I did not purpose to write a national hymn. I laid the song aside and nearly forgot I had made it. Some weeks later I sent it to Mr. Mason, and on the following Fourth of July he brought it out, much to my surprise, at a children's celebration in the Park Street Church, Boston."

Four years later the song was published in a collection and soon caught the public fancy. Today the hymn is sung wherever there are loyal Americans.

> My country! 'tis of thee, sweet land of liberty, of thee I sing:
> Land where my fathers died! Land of the pilgrims' pride!
> From every mountain side let freedom ring!
>
> My native country, thee, land of the noble free, thy name I love;
> I love thy rocks and rills, thy woods and templed hills:
> My heart with rapture thrills like that above.
>
> Let music swell the breeze, and ring from all the trees sweet
> freedom's song: Let mortal tongues awake; let all that breathe
> partake; Let rocks their silence break, the sound prolong.
>
> Our father's God to Thee, Author of liberty, to Thee we sing:
> Long may our land be bright with freedom's holy light; Protect
> us by Thy might, great God, our King!

YANKEE DOODLE

American Indians called the English colonists "Yenghees," the nearest they could come to saying, "Anglais," the French word for "English." The tune, "Yankee Doodle," came to the colonies from England where, under Oliver Cromwell, it had been sung by the Cavaliers to make fun of the Puritans.

The first American version of the song is supposed to have been written by a physician in General Braddock's army during the French and Indian War. Although it made fun of them, the good-natured colonists soon appropriated it for themselves and it has been a favorite American air ever since.

Father and I went down to camp, Along with Captain Gooding;
And there we see the men and boys As thick as hasty pudding.

CHORUS

Yankee Doodle keep it up, Yankee Doodle dandy.
Mind the music and the step, And with the girls be handy.

And there was Captain Washington, Upon a slapping stallion,
A giving orders to his men; I guess there was a million.

And then the feathers on his hat, They looked so very fine, ah!
I wanted peskily to get To give to my Jemima.

And there I see a swamping gun, Large as a log of maple, Upon
a mighty little cart; A load for father's cattle.

And every time they fired it off, It took a horn of powder; It
made a noise like father's gun, Only a nation louder.

The troopers, too, would gallop up And fire right in our faces;
It scared me almost half to death To see them run such races.

It scared me so I hooked it off, Nor stopped, as I remember, Nor
turned about till I got home, Locked up in mother's chamber.

THE BATTLE HYMN OF THE REPUBLIC

"John Brown's Body" was the popular song in the North in 1861, and Mrs. Julia Ward Howe wrote her stirring words to the same air. While watching a review of Union troops near Washington and listening to the soldiers sing the "John Brown" song, a friend had suggested that she should write some words worthy of the tune.

That same night Mrs. Howe awoke to find the words of "The Battle Hymn of the Republic" forming in her mind. She hastily wrote them down before she could forget them. They were published soon afterward in the "Atlantic Monthly," and soon all the North was singing them. The first time Abraham Lincoln heard the new song, he cried out, with tears in his eyes, "Sing it again."

> Mine eyes have seen the glory of the coming of the Lord: He is trampling out the vintage where the grapes of wrath are stored; He hath loosed the fateful lightning of his terrible swift sword: His truth is marching on.
>
> I have seen him in the watch-fires of a hundred circling camps; They have builded him an altar in the evening dews and damps; I can read his righteous sentence by the dim and flaring lamps: His day is marching on.
>
> I have read a fiery gospel, writ in burnished rows of steel: "As ye deal with my contemners, so with you my grace shall deal; Let the Hero, born of woman, crush the serpent with his heel, Since God is marching on."
>
> He has sounded forth the trumpet that shall never call retreat; He is sifting out the hearts of men before his judgment-seat: O, be swift, my soul, to answer him! be jubilant, my feet! Our God is marching on.

In the beauty of the lilies Christ was born across the sea, With a glory in his bosom that transfigures you and me; As he died to make men holy, let us die to make men free, While God is marching on.

AMERICA THE BEAUTIFUL

Katharine Lee Bates, then an instructor in Wellesley College, was on her first trip west when she wrote "America the Beautiful." In Chicago where she had stopped to see the Columbian Exposition, she had been much impressed by the beauty of the white buildings, and she had spent several weeks "under the purple range of the Rocky Mountains." It was a wonderful moment when she stood on Pike's Peak and looked out over the wide expanse of surrounding country, and it was then she thought of the first words for her beautiful hymn.

O beautiful for spacious skies,
For amber waves of grain,
For purple mountain majesties
Above the fruited plain!
America! America!
God shed his grace on thee
And crown thy good with brotherhood
From sea to shining sea!

O beautiful for pilgrim feet
Whose stern, impassioned stress
A thoroughfare for freedom beat
Across the wilderness!
America! America!
God mend thine every flaw,
Confirm thy soul in self-control,
Thy liberty in law!

O beautiful for heroes proved
In liberating strife,
Who more than self their country loved
And mercy more than life!
America! America!
May God thy gold refine
Till all success be nobleness
And every gain divine!

O beautiful for patriot dream
That sees beyond the years
Thine alabaster cities gleam
Undimmed by human tears!
America! America!
God shed his grace on thee
And crown thy good with brotherhood
From sea to shining sea!

Days of National Remembrance

I AM AN AMERICAN. I patriotically observe these American holidays.

MARTIN LUTHER KING JR. DAY
Third Monday in January

First observed as a federal holiday in 1986, following legislation signed into law in 1983. It honors the birthday and legacy of Dr. Martin Luther King Jr., a leader of the American civil rights movement.

LINCOLN'S BIRTHDAY
February 12

First observed in 1866, ten months after Abraham Lincoln's death. While never established as a federal holiday, it has been recognized as a legal or ceremonial holiday in several states.

WASHINGTON'S BIRTHDAY
Third Monday in February

First observed in Newport, R.I., on February 11, 1781, while George Washington was still living. According to the Old Style Calendar in use at that time, Washington had been born on February 11. After the adoption of the New Style

Calendar, the date was changed to February 22. Officially titled Washington's Birthday, it is a federal holiday and is commonly known as Presidents' Day.

ARBOR DAY
Date determined by each state

First observed in Nebraska on April 10, 1872, encouraging the planting and care of trees. Today, Arbor Day is recognized in all states, though the date varies by region and climate.

PAN-AMERICAN DAY
April 14

Established in 1931 to commemorate April 14, 1889, when the Commercial Bureau of the American Republics was formed, later becoming the Pan-American Union. It recognizes cooperation among the nations of the Americas and is observed by proclamation.

CHILD HEALTH DAY
First Monday in October

First observed in 1924 and formally recognized by a Congressional resolution in 1928. It is proclaimed annually by the President to promote the health and well-being of children.

MOTHER'S DAY
Second Sunday in May

Established nationally in 1914 by joint resolution of Congress and signed by President Woodrow Wilson. The holiday originated through the efforts of Anna Jarvis, who sought to honor her mother.

MEMORIAL DAY (Decoration Day)
Last Monday in May

First observed in Columbus, Georgia, April 26, 1866. Two years later, General John A. Logan, commander-in-chief of the Grand Army of the Republic, set aside May 30 for "decorating the graves of comrades who died in defense of their country during the late rebellion." Memorial Day honors those who died in military service to the United States. It became a federal holiday and was moved to the last Monday in May in 1971.

FLAG DAY
June 14

Commemorates the adoption of the United States flag on June 14, 1777. First widely observed in the late 19th century. Flag Day is recognized by presidential proclamation.

JUNETEENTH
June 19

Marks June 19, 1865, when enslaved people in Texas learned of their freedom following the Civil War.

FATHER'S DAY
Third Sunday in June

First celebrated June 19, 1910 – the idea of Mrs. John Bruce Dodd. It was sponsored by the Ministerial Association and the Y.M.C.A. of Washington, D.C.

INDEPENDENCE DAY
July 4

Commemorates the adoption of the Declaration of Independence in 1776.

LABOR DAY
First Monday in September

Established in 1894 through the American labor movement. Recognizes the contributions of workers.

COLUMBUS DAY
Second Monday in October

Originally observed in New York City in 1792 to mark the 300th anniversary of Christopher Columbus's landing.

VETERANS DAY
November 11

Originally commemorating the end of the First World War, Armistice Day became an official holiday in 1921, the year the American Unknown Soldier was buried in Washington. By act of Congress, it became a federal holiday in 1938. Today, it honors all U.S. military veterans.

THANKSGIVING DAY
Fourth Thursday in November

First observed December 13, 1621, in Plymouth Colony by the Pilgrims to express their gratitude to God for a bountiful harvest. In 1789, November 26 was set aside by President George Washington as a day of national Thanksgiving. In 1862, through the efforts of Mrs. Sarah Josepha Hale, President Lincoln proclaimed the last Thursday in November as an annual national holiday.

Today, Thanksgiving is a federal holiday observed in all fifty states and every territory and possession of the United States.

Part Five

THE AMERICAN LEGACY

What History Has Handed Down

A Legacy Received
A Responsibility Inherited

I AM AN AMERICAN. I give thanks for and praise America's glorious history.

The history of the United States is not merely a record of political events or territorial growth. It is the account of a people who believed that liberty was not granted by kings, but endowed by Almighty God.

Long before independence was declared, men and women crossed oceans fleeing tyranny, convinced that freedom of conscience was worth any cost. They believed, as George Washington later wrote, that "the propitious smiles of Heaven can never be expected on a nation that disregards the eternal rules of order and right which Heaven itself has ordained."

On July 4, 1776, America's founders announced to the world a principle unprecedented in its successful application: that all men are created equal, endowed by their Creator with unalienable rights—among them life, liberty, and the pursuit of happiness. This was not a rejection of God's authority, but an appeal to it. As Thomas Jefferson affirmed, the liberties of a nation rest on "the laws of nature and of nature's God."

The cost of this declaration was immense. Freedom was consecrated by sacrifice, sealed by blood, and defended by ordinary citizens who believed the cause of liberty was worth their lives.

In 1787, a new experiment in self-government took shape. The Constitution of the United States established a government deriving its just powers from the consent of the governed, restrained by law, divided in authority, and accountable to the people. John Adams was clear-eyed about its foundation: "Our Constitution was made only for a moral and religious people. It is wholly inadequate to the government of any other."

That Constitution endured its greatest trial during the Civil War, when the nation was torn apart over slavery and secession. From 1861 to 1865, the Union was preserved at tremendous cost. Abraham Lincoln, reflecting on the conflict, acknowledged divine judgment and human responsibility alike, believing the nation was being tested— and refined. The abolition of slavery marked not only a political victory, but a moral reckoning.

As the nation grew, it expanded its borders through treaties, purchases, and settlement: Louisiana in 1803, Florida in 1819, Texas in 1845, Oregon in 1846, California and the Southwest in 1848, Alaska in 1867, and the Panama Canal Zone in the early twentieth century. With growth came opportunity—and obligation—to steward liberty wisely.

The twentieth century brought new trials. Americans confronted global tyranny in two world wars, resisted totalitarianism during the Cold War, and advanced civil rights at home, striving to more fully live out the principles proclaimed at the nation's founding. The space race, the fall of the Iron Curtain, and the peaceful transitions of power reaffirmed America's unique role as a defender of freedom on the world stage.

The twenty-first century has tested the nation again—through acts of terror, cultural division, economic uncertainty, and global instability. Yet the American experiment endures, not because it is perfect, but because its foundation is strong.

Ronald Reagan once warned, "Freedom is never more than one generation away from extinction. It must be fought for, protected, and handed on." Liberty is not self-sustaining. It depends on citizens who understand its source, cherish its cost, and accept its responsibility.

This book records what has been entrusted to us: ideas, documents, traditions, sacrifices, and faith. The question now rests with the reader.

Will the light of liberty dim—or will it be carried forward?

The beacon of freedom has been passed from generation to generation. It now rests in your hands. Take up the mantle. Guard what was won. Teach what was given. And ensure that the blessings of liberty endure—for this nation, and for all who look to its example.

www.ingramcontent.com/pod-product-compliance
Lightning Source LLC
Chambersburg PA
CBHW051626120626
46551CB00014B/1950